CHRISTOPHER
AND GAY

CHRISTOPHER AND GAY

A *Partisan's View of the*
Greenwich Village Homosexual Scene

Wallace Hamilton

Saturday Review Press

NEW YORK

Published simultaneously in Canada by
Doubleday Canada Ltd., Toronto.

Library of Congress Catalog Card Number: 72–94798

ISBN 0–8415–0243–9

Saturday Review Press
380 Madison Avenue
New York, New York 10017

PRINTED IN THE UNITED STATES OF AMERICA

Design by Tere LoPrete

For the tribe, with love

CHRISTOPHER
AND GAY

Chapter One

The letter was postmarked Pittsburgh. Opening it, I found it came from Cory.[1] In Pittsburgh? Cory rarely got out of New York City, and his usual mode of contact was a gentle but authoritative knock on the door at four in the morning after a heavy night on downs and liquor. But the letter from Pittsburgh announced that he had left New York City and joined a group called "The Children of God."

"I know you must be scratching your head, trying to figure this one out," he wrote, "no more than I do at times. It is such an abrupt about-face that it must surely seem strange, and sometimes it even seems so to me. Yet I know that this is what I have been waiting for most of my life. What do I mean, 'most of my life'? I mean *all* of

[1]Personal names are changed. The one exception is Sal, whose name was highly publicized in the press. All place names are unchanged.

my life. I have always yearned to belong. I have always
wanted to know God and abide in his Love. I just never
could see a way to do it before. So many little things that
have troubled me, which are important to me only because I noticed them and caused me to question something or someone, are now answered for me. I can see
that I have been walking toward my present place for a
long time."

Cory would not be Cory if he didn't ask for something
—money for carfare, money for cigarettes. I could almost hear that short intake of breath that usually
preceded the pitch. But this pitch was something else
again. He wanted a three-by-five-inch copy of the King
James Version of the Bible, "so I can carry it at all times."
He also asked me to get his birth certificate so that he
could qualify for a passport because "The Lord may have
it in mind to send me to Europe someday." A simple
statement followed. "I am Paul Mandor. My father was
Michael Mandor. My mother was Julia Creston. I was
born at Metropolitan Hospital in New York City on July
10, 1940."

Pau. Mandor. I had known Cory for a long year about
as well as anyone, and this was the first time I had known
his name. Out of all the welter of fantasies and identities,
there emerged, as a vital statistic on file at the Bureau of
Records, one Paul Mandor. But the phrasing was as
much a revelation as the name itself. Not "I was born
Paul Mandor." Or "I was first named Paul Mandor." But
a straight "I am Paul Mandor," with all other identities
sloughed off. It seemed almost an embarrassing intimacy
that I was to take to the Bureau of Records, while leaving
Cory's street identity preserved as "little Cory James, the
down freak."

It was quite an identity, a self-dramatization that could
hold its own on the nether reaches of Christopher Street,
where I first met him at Old Danny's Bar in March of

1971. I was rigged in a cap, pea jacket, denims, and boots, looking as if I had just shipped in from Hong Kong and had keel-hauled a few of the crew along the way. In fact, I'd just arrived in town a month or two before, had yet to establish my social bearings where I wanted them, and was plain lonely. At the other end of the bar, in full regalia, was Cory. Dark brown hair flowing below his shoulders, chain after chain around his neck with pendants gleaming, bracelet after bracelet on both arms, a shirt open to the navel, skin-tight pants, and boots up to his knees. He was short and slim. His face was opulent, with heavy eyebrows and full lips, and to complete the madness of his presence—sidewhiskers. I observed this phenomenon from a safe distance, braced against the cigarette machine and holding my beer can like a security blanket. I was Discovering the Village, Stalking the Gay Underworld, and Observing Life. Of course if, in the toils of this process, I could find somebody to go to bed with, that would be good, too. But since I had enhanced a normally forbidding presence with a lot of somber, seaworthy blackness, I could only expect to scare the living hell out of anyone within ten feet.

Except Cory.

I was minding my own business when I felt someone come between me and the cigarette machine. Turning, I discovered The Phenomenon, his face six inches from mine, an odor of body sweat and incense, and a measured, reedy, aristocratic voice asking "Would you by any chance have the money for a brandy?" I allowed as maybe I had money for one. That's how it all began.

In retrospect, it is clear that that one contact with Cory determined just about everyone I was to know in the next year or so. Cory was a street freak; he knew a lot of other street freaks, and they in turn knew others. The people Cory brought around brought others, and they, others, unto the seventh generation. With Cory I entered one of the social enclaves in the gay subculture. But only one of many. I keep wondering what would have happened if that first contact had not been Cory, but one of those long, lean, languid Beautiful People from the Upper East Side who might have led me into the world of fashion, theater, decoration, and the outer reaches of High Culture. I'm not sure how long I'd have lasted, but it might have been interesting for a while. Or that first meeting might have been with some intense intellectual from the Upper West Side, in which case I'd have spent a good deal of time and money running up and down on the subways to Morningside Heights, earnestly reading the *New York Review of Books* on the train, just to make sure I knew what everyone was talking about that week. Or I might have met one of those discreet monied types from Scarsdale, or a stalwart academic from Rutgers, or an artist from SoHo (the South-of-Houston-Street arts enclave below Greenwich Village). Each of them would have been an entry into a distinctive part of the gay subculture with its own social context, its own customs and mores, its own gathering places. Sure, there was plenty of communication among the various parts of the subculture, and any component could give some illumination to the whole. But with Cory I happened to enter the subculture through a particular gate. If I had entered through another gate, this would be a very different book, based on very different experiences.

At any rate, Cory got his brandy, and I started getting my education. During preliminary, rather formal chitchat, I had a chance to size up a man who, from the looks of him, might have stepped out of a Warhol movie. His eyes were big, dark, and they looked at me straight-on and unblinking like the eyes of a child. His talk was slow, deliberate, and he had a delicate wit, punctuated with chuckles that began deep in his chest. Nor did he take himself with any particular seriousness. Rattling his pendants and bracelets, he shrugged—"After all, a boy's got to wear some . . . thing"—leaving the general impression that all the metalwork was the most reasonable alternative to a full coat of chain armor. A mere shirt and pants were obviously beyond the pale.

As the alcoholic haze thickened around us, I felt the pressure of his shoulder against my side and sensed that the preliminaries were over. I suggested we go to my place. He suggested we go to his place. Since I was no little fascinated by the chance to explore the native habitat of this phenomenon, I said okay and off we reeled into the night streets. It was a difficult journey because the streets kept moving under our feet, but we managed to end up in some large dank tenement on Bayard Street. The stairs were as uncertain as the streets, but they eventually led to a third-floor pad that was Cory's habitat. Its three small rooms had little furniture except for a mattress on the floor, some chests and chairs of uncertain vintage, and a television set. But the room with the mattress was draped with aluminum foil that glinted against some colored lights and the flicker of the television. On one wall was a massive painting of a male face with eyes that fixed attention like the Ancient Mariner.

Three figures—two hulking long-haired men and a woman—were strewn about the bedroom, silent and passive, watching the television set. The movie was *Ben Hur*, with Charlton Heston. Cory introduced me airily and proceeded to take off all his clothes, but there was no competing with a chariot race. Torpor lay thick in the room, an environment out of Gorky with psychedelic trimmings. All that really moved was on the screen, shadows against the stillness. Yet when Cory, wrapped in some flowing white thing, deposited himself on the mattress, the bodies slowly rearranged themselves like iron filings around a magnet.

The girl in the group was Linda, sometime addict, hooker, and fag-hag.[2] She had short dark hair, a well-molded face, an opulent figure, and on the night in question she was spaced out of her mind.

The chariot race ended and the film lumbered on to the Crucifixion. The heavens opened and the rains descended on the just and unjust, including Ben Hur's mother and sister who had been afflicted with leprosy. The rain effected a miraculous cure and the women held up their hands, made whole again in the power of the Lord. Linda stared at the screen. "See, the rain washed it all away," she said. "They're all clean now. The rain washed it all away." The sound of her voice hung in the stillness. No one moved. No one responded. "The rain made them all clean again."

In a few moments, there was an uproar in the living room caused by a booming voice of uncertain sex, which sounded as if it were announcing either the end of the world or a Russian invasion. The owner of the voice appeared at the bedroom door, arms flung high in the sheer drama of the occasion. "Wanda is here!" the voice announced. "And all you motherfuckers better know it!"

Well . . . it wasn't the end of the world. It wasn't even a Russian invasion. But it was a Wanda entrance. I hadn't seen a better one since Tallulah Bankhead. Behind her was a straight-arrow type with close-cropped hair and a chino jacket who came into the bedroom on Wanda's wake. The others in the room began to move, respond, and gather energy from her. She had brought in the street, the night's affairs, the reality of the city, and, with a kind of bizarre hyperbole, broke through the shells of private fantasy that had shut the city out. Her voice went on and on like a tocsin, describing the excursions and alarms of being cruised in the subway, getting thrown

[2]"Fag-hag" is affectionate gay parlance for a woman who likes to socialize with gay men.

out of a gay bar, getting chased by a cop, trying to find her dealer, and instead finding . . . an ecstatic pause and an arm flung around the shoulder of the straight-arrow . . . Benny. "That is your name, isn't it, Benny? It's so cute!"

Benny blushed. The perfumes of Araby and the langors of the Kasbah were obviously in store for Benny, and he radiated anticipation.

Wanda was a queen of brash Auntie Mame femininity. Slight, dark-haired, with a chiseled face, she could wear ordinary male clothes and still come on as womanhood personified. She was a queen who didn't need drag. Yet she was a he and, as I was to find out later to my considerable bemusement, a male chauvinist pig to the core. Wanda was a man who liked men, and if the way to get men was to camp it up in a queenly fashion, camp it up he would for the straight-arrow Bennys of the world, and whatever happened in bed thereafter was . . . well, the fortunes of pickups. Wanda managed.

That night he was going to manage Benny. Just who was going to manage with who else in the contingent in the bedroom was uncertain. Arms and legs began to make contact in a slow minuet of positioning that presaged entwinements of exquisite complexity. I wasn't sure I was ready for all that; the people in the room just didn't turn me on that much. Then I heard Cory's voice, close to my ear: "I'll be over to see you in a few days." I nodded, delicately extricated myself from the gathering storm on the mattress, and wended my way home to solitude and sleep.

It wasn't exactly a promising beginning. Still, I went to sleep feeling peaceful. I had a hunch it was going to work out. But then, *what* was going to "work out"? Just what was I out to prove, or discover, or settle? I had spent most of my life as an active, enthusiastic, and sometimes rampageous straight, with only occasional short-lived gay interludes. Compared to life with women, those interludes seemed strangely pallid and restrained. Yet the memory of them persisted: not the memory of sexuality but of maleness, the very special relaxation of being with one's own kind. Straight life was great and all that, but the stretch of past and future could make the present vibrate with a tension to shudder the spirit. With a male, there was no past or future, just the comfort of the transcendent now. No history or expectancies, powers, or principalities. Just . . . us . . . now, in the consciousness of our kindred maleness, and the caring that could come of kinship.

That was the memory. And it would not go away. In fact, each new episode enhanced it. It was almost as if all the parts of me had sat around a conference table all my life making decisions that systematically ignored and gave short shrift to the gay part of me, while that gay part kept pounding the table and saying, "Gentlemen, like it or not, I'm here." The other parts kept saying, with growing fatigue and irritation, "Yes, we know you're here, but just sit over there in the corner and keep quiet. And, for heaven's sake, don't *do* anything!" But the gay part of me refused to go sit in the corner, kept its place at the conference table, and at last became so insistent that all the other parts finally turned, looked at that noisome thing, and in a chorus said, "All right, goddamnit, go *do it!*"

The trouble was that after all the *Sturm und Drang* the gay part of me didn't have that clear an idea of just what to do. So when I'd go down to Old Danny's, which was the only gay bar I knew in New York, and stand by the cigarette machine and stare, all the other parts of me would be hooting their heads off about the big deal that the gay part of me had gotten into. Cory was, at least, *something*.

Cory showed up at the apartment after dinner a few days later, in chains, pendants, bracelets, and a mirrored jacket of many colors and East Indian origins. But also boots, and still the side-whiskers. He kissed me, sat down, and asked for a drink. The lights were low. The candles in the fireplace reflected in the mirrors of his jacket. Drink in hand, Cory started talking. The voice was soft-textured, but the words were precise, and they flowed almost endlessly. Cory was Rumanian, with Gypsy blood, and as the words and fantasies and stories rolled on, I felt transported into a hut in the Transylvanian mountains and the firelight evoked a hundred myths and mysteries. Not that Count Dracula was any near neighbor, nor were the werewolves at the door. But they were . . . suggested . . . along with beautiful maidens, gallant knights, and stretches of flowered mountain meadows.

But this was no idle story-spinning; there was a particular intensity about his eyes as they held mine, an urgency when my eyes or attention wandered. Cory, it was evident, had found someone who was not so constantly stoned that he could not listen, comprehend, and respond. The discovery opened the floodgates of his memory and imagination: scraps of old movie stories, science fiction he had read, poems he had composed, people he had known, and a long recital of the woes and wonders of Marilyn Monroe. The words, ideas, and images tumbled out in a confusion that defied sequence or order but was hypnotic in its swirling variety.

After the second drink, Cory slowly took off his boots and stretched back in the chair. His talk gradually shifted tenor. We were no longer in the Transylvanian mountains, but back in New York City. I heard about how he was born in Yorkville, left home at fifteen, lived on the streets, pimping, hustling, robbing, endured a stretch on Riker's Island, a stretch on skag, got and lost jobs, went back to robbing, got into street fights and achieved some victories—the whole turmoil revealed in meticulous diction. But there was a bravado about it that didn't quite ring true. It all could have happened, and probably did, but that wasn't what he was saying. Something about his eyes, big and staring . . .

He closed in. "Everything I do, I do for money." Pause. He let the statement hang. "It has to be that way."

I suggested he go do it someplace else, that it was not the route I went, and most especially not the route I was going to go with him.

Another pause. Slowly Cory put on his boots. He stood up, thanked me for the drink, and headed toward the door. Halfway to the door he hesitated, turned, circled the couch on which I was sitting, hesitated again, lay down on the couch, his head in my lap. He said nothing. I said nothing. The candles flickered. Finally he said, "Let's go to bed." And we did. And it was beautiful.

A couple of weeks later the arrangement was formalized when Cory left his apartment in the tender care of the resident freaks, packed his chains and bracelets and violet shirts and purple pants and mirrored jackets, and moved in. Then's when I began to learn a few things, a process that continues. . . .

Chapter Two

When Cory came out, at the age of fifteen, in the mid-1950s, nobody had ever heard of "Gay Liberation" or "Women's Liberation." Nor was the public particularly aware of "Black Liberation," although Martin Luther King was stirring that awareness with the Montgomery bus strike. Most gays were locked securely in their respective closets and when they moved in general society, they did so invisibly.

But Cory was an up-front queen and, like blacks, clearly visible. As he was to say later, "We never came out. We were out there all the time." What Cory was "out" in was a gay underworld, feral, furtive, geared to raw survival by any means, fair or foul. The surcease was alcohol and drugs. That was life, accepted for what it was on the assumption that it would never change.

We can speculate on the effect that television coverage

of the civil rights movement of the 1960s had on those young up-front gays. They knew what those nightsticks and police dogs felt like. They also saw blacks standing their ground in an assertion of their blackness. The phrase "Black Is Beautiful" is a true precursor of "Gay Is Proud," and it is not difficult to see the similarities between that sit-in that took place at a lunch counter in Greensboro, North Carolina, in 1960 and the "Stonewall Riots" of 1969. Both events, prosaic in and of themselves, turned out to be landmarks of liberation. Each was a place and time when people, in exasperation, broke out of old habits of action, and by some process of internal liberation asserted their identity and the dignity of that identity.

In 1969, the Stonewall was a gay bar on Sheridan Square in New York City. Like many other gay bars, it was subjected to periodic harassing raids by the police. According to time-honored custom, the patrons and staff of a gay bar were loaded into paddy wagons, taken down to the precinct house, given a rough time, and then released. It was a convenient way of keeping the police force well occupied and undistracted by such incidentals as muggings, rapings, shootings, and burglaries that might be occurring in the neighborhood.

But that summer night at the Stonewall the gays didn't go their docile way into the paddy wagons; they fought back. For several nights thereafter, gay after gay came "out of the closet and into the streets" in a display of "Gay Power" the likes of which had ne'er been seen. The annual Christopher Street parades up Sixth Avenue in June commemorate that event.

The Stonewall Riots were, to hard-core gays like Cory, simply a public confirmation of a process of internal liberation long since at work. But they could walk with their heads a little higher, and feel a richer sense of territorial possession. "The streets," Cory would say with a flash in his eye, "are *mine.*" As if to prove it, he stopped me one evening under a lamp post at the corner of Christopher Street and Seventh Avenue. "Kiss me," he commanded.

Well, I was out of the closet and all that, but the corner of *Seventh Avenue and Christopher* with traffic going by like there was no tomorrow . . .?

"Here?" I said.

"Here," he said.

Fully expecting the Tactical Police Force to descend en masse, I did.

It was a post-Stonewall scene.

Cory and I were hooked on each other, and for that matter still are. But we had our cultural problems. For one thing, I had this weird habit of wanting to go to bed at night and get up in the morning. I liked my denim plain, thank you, and please omit the lavender scarf. I didn't know how to cruise; all I knew how to do was glower, imperiously. I'd be damned if I'd speak to anyone to whom I had not been formally introduced by a mutual friend. And my taste in gay bars was tired Old Danny's down near the Christopher Street waterfront. I was, in Cory's terms, pretty hopeless.

Wanda, the resplendent drag-queen I'd first met over at Cory's Bayard Street place, used to drop by the house periodically and sized up the situation in her worldly way. I was sitting there one evening, giving out with my usual winsome grunts and glowers, when Wanda turned to Cory, her hand gesturing to me as she might to a Neanderthal skull. "You want 'em butch. So . . . you got him butch," she said. "What do you care if he looks like he just got off a tugboat, as long as he's good in bed?" Wanda had a clear sense of priorities.

But Cory decided my ignorance could somehow be ameliorated by an exploration of his various haunts south of Fourteenth Street (and Cory had done a lot of haunting). Which was okay with me as long as we got home by one or so. I was interested in observing the flora and fauna of this adopted world.

One night we went to some particularly vibrant establishment over on Second Avenue around midnight. Cory had one drink and proceeded to get lost. Twelve-thirty came and went, and Cory was still lost somewhere in a swirl of dancing figures. Came one, and still no Cory. I walked out in high dudgeon, with an equally high blood-level of alcohol, and stalked home alone to find Wanda sitting on the doorstep. By some complex prior arrangement, Cory was meeting Wanda at the house and they, in turn, were going out for a second round on the town. What I should have done, of course, was go out on the town with Wanda and leave Cory to his just deserts. But I was in a fit of dominant-culture moral indignation that would countenance no such obvious solution. Cory, goddamn him, had walked out on me, and, to add insult to injury, was planning on walking out again for some dissolute lolly-gagging around with Wanda.

By the time Cory floated in—adrift on downs—a half hour later, I was ready to let fly. I guess neither Cory nor Wanda had ever heard the likes of my harangue. It brooked no argument, suffered no contradiction. They just stood there, and then, without a word, Cory closed the front door behind him and fled into the darkness.

At that moment I learned something. I would have thought that Wanda, as Cory's friend, would have hurried out after him. But no. Wanda stayed to keep the relationship intact until the storm blew over. As friends, they worked in tandem to maintain whatever security might have been established. Amid the ephemerality of the gay world, a contact that held some promise of stability was to be preserved by any means at hand. So Wanda put his body there, a slim tense hesitant thing, to keep the territoriality. The next day, when Cory came back, Wanda disappeared.

A few weeks later, Cory elected to become Virgil to my Dante in an exploration of the various infernal circles of the East Village. We ended up at what was then the Hippodrome. Cory latched onto his one drink and disappeared. He'd learned something, though. Every fifteen minutes or so he checked back to see if I was still there. I sat at the bar with some middle-aged accountant-looking type: glasses, thinning hair, business suit, the works. He just didn't look right on Avenue A. In response to my delicate inquiry: "Oh, I don't know, I just sit here to see what comes along." I had visions of the poor guy sitting there at three or four in the morning, still waiting. . . . God knows what the accounts receivable would look like the next day.

Cory hauled in his catch for the evening with all the triumph of a man landing a striped bass—more properly, two striped bass. One was a slight muscular kid of twenty or so with a face off the streets and a happy, shaggy-dog personality. His name was Bruce. With him was a beautiful blonde who looked like a runaway girl from Englewood, New Jersey. Cory had decided that this was just the sort of thing to take back to his orgiastic friends on Bayard Street. I decided that matters might be a little less appalling for them in the West Village, and furthermore there was liquor at home. To the West Village we went.

Seated in the living room, we had a refined social occasion. With a newly met girl around, gay households tend to get rather formal, and the social amenities, along with the liquor, flowed gently in the night. The social amenities got a little frayed when Bruce passed out, and they got even more frayed when Cory passed out. There we were, the blonde and I, looking at each other. My heterosexual impulses surged with adolescent fervor, and I moved with a Charles Boyer authority to fulfill them.

His name, as it turned out, was Quincy. I'm sure Charles Boyer would have been as surprised as I was.

Bruce and Quincy had an eighteen-hour passion of smoldering intensity and acrobatic ingenuity. Then Quincy retreated to the wilds of Massachusetts. Bruce stayed. Which seemed rather curious since Bruce, bereft of Quincy, announced to the world that he was going straight.

With Cory in residence and Bruce using the place as a base for some rather wide-ranging operations, something approximating a household began to develop, and with it a bewildering counterpoint of roles and kinship patterns. In my relationships with Cory he could be shaman, son, wife, lover, friend, adversary, and plain shrew. As a guide to the gay world, he was also no mean teacher. His roles were not defined in any self-conscious "now, I'm going to be this" way, but I could tell pretty clearly which role he was playing at any given time. He could slip from one to the next with grace and no particular sense of effort. Cory had been around.

Bruce, on the other hand, who was ten years or more younger than Cory, had been brought up by a mother and various stepfathers, legal and otherwise, in small towns in Pennsylvania. Because of this mobility of location and family patterns, he could cope with surrogate relationships with comparative ease, but his responses were limited. Bruce played the Happy Kid. Or sometimes, with his simian prizefighter's stance and build, he played the Happy Chimp. (No idle affinity, this. Sometime later I was with him at the Bronx Zoo when he was tripping, and he went into transports over a family of gorillas until he developed a passion for a white rhino. I was lucky to get him out of there.)

The Happy Kid role stood him in very good stead. He could get around me with alarming speed and efficiency. He could pick up anyone, anywhere, and would usually bring him home at strange hours. If I didn't like it, he would smile his happy smile and snuggle winsomely.

The little bastard. In a sense, he had returned to child-hood, with a mommy (Cory), a daddy (me), and a replenished supply of blueberry yoghurt. Which was fine by him, but not so fine by Cory, who didn't quite dig being the Great American Mom. From time to time Cory would get quite shrewish about it, and Bruce, wounded, would retire to the arms of a bevy of black drag-queens at some hotel on Eighth Street. The drag-queens would salve his wounds with an ego-satisfying flutter over his lily-white flesh and he'd be back in a day or so, smiling as happily as ever. Cory would have simmered down sufficiently for life in the household to go on for a while without uproar.

All this took place in the dear dead days when Christopher's End was one of the great gay bars in the city. Bruce had found it, with unerring instinct, within twenty-four hours after he hit town. In the course of time he became one of the stable of male go-go dancers there who were hired to stir the gonads of those senior engineers and vice presidents in charge of sales from New Jersey who habituated the place. They lurked in the dark corners as the lights flooded the dancing platform where some lissome young thing went through provocations from the Greek. Bruce wasn't very good at it, but he had a body that wouldn't quit and the special attention of one of the factotums of the place.

Christopher's End was a happy gay bar with a large central room that housed the bar and dance floor. One side room held the pool table. The other could hold an overflow crowd, but was usually darkened and served as a "Back Room." The Back Room was an arcane practice that has since, apparently, gone out of fashion in Village bars. In its heyday, it was a walled-off area, pitch-black, adjacent to the bar, that served as an arena for any variety of catch-as-catch-can sex. Sometimes two guys would meet at the bar and, after preliminaries, repair to the Back Room to do their thing. In other cases, singles who

had not had much luck at the bar or pool table would
drift into the Back Room and wait for a body—any body
—to find them in the darkness. The whole idea of such
utterly depersonalized sex struck me as barbaric, but
what closed down the Village back rooms was not fastidi-
ousness, but the rumor of a "Mad Slasher" who was said
to go around from one back room to another playing
havoc on penile musculatures with a razor blade.

At any rate, the Back Room at Christopher's End, in
contrast to some other Village gay bars, had no great
significance. Christopher's End was a place for socializing, usually among friends. A high proportion of the
people who patronized the place knew each other and
every night was Old Home Week. Linda, Cory's friend
whom I had met over at the Bayard Street pad, worked
there when she wasn't doing her stint of hooking. As a
fag-hag in good standing, she moved in the environment, playing her roles as waitress and social director
with genial authority. If people weren't friends when
they came into Christopher's End, Linda set out to
remedy the situation. She felt it was just plain foolish for
all those nice young guys to stand around staring at each
other without *doing* anything about it. So Linda *did* something about it. I'd be sitting in a corner grumping about
the state of the nation with some other butch type and
Linda would come up to tell me that she'd found me
some gorgeous boy who was terribly lonely and whom I
had to meet. I would tell her I had my hands full with
Cory, and all of Cory's friends, and Bruce, and all the
flotsam and jetsam that Bruce dragged in. She'd give me
a big kiss and go off, Elsa Maxwell fashion, to find some
other companionship for her gorgeous lonely boy.

Another denizen of Christopher's End was Quincy, the
blond queen who had first shown up at the apartment
with Bruce and subsequently retreated to Massachusetts.
His home hearth turned out to be a bore, so back he

came to the city to hitch up with Burt, who was one of
the managers of the place.

Burt was a lanky, Honest-John looking guy who, under
other circumstances, could pass for an English teacher at
a prep school or a customers' man on Wall Street. Burt
was a harried man. The pressures of keeping the bar
stocked and assuaging various temperaments around the
place were considerable. The pressures of keeping
Quincy were even worse. When Burt and I would go off
to a corner of the pool room to commiserate with each
other about our hard lives with our respective lovers, the
conversation might have been recorded at the Biltmore
Men's Bar.

"What she's got to understand," said Burt, "is that this
is a tough job and I have to keep my mind on it." He
shook his head. "But all she wants to do is go somewhere
else. And I got to be *here*. And Monday nights I'm tired
and I want to stay home. Can't make her understand that.
Then there's this sex thing. I mean, *she's* tired. So I say,
all right, go back and see your mother in Massachusetts.
Oh no, says she, you're just trying to get rid of me so you
can tomcat all those chickens. So I tell her no I'm not
trying to get rid of her, I just think the change might do
her good, you know, get her less *tired* or whatever it is.
I have to get my rocks off somehow. So then she goes
into this big liquor thing, that if I wasn't so drunk all the
time and not able to get it up and all, she wouldn't be so
tired. And I'm saying if she wasn't so tired, I *could* get it
up. And round and round we go." He sighs a heavy sigh.
"And that's how I get tired."

Sometimes it was Quincy who dished the tea. "So, with
his drinking all the time, what can I do? I mean, there's
no romance, you know what I mean? He just piles into
bed grunting and groaning and bitching about the liquor
deliveries and tells me to roll over. Just like that. I mean,
what does he think, I don't have feelings or anything? So

I tell him I'm tired, and then he gets mad and tells me
I should go to Massachusetts." He sighs a heavy sigh.
"And I love him. And I try to make a good wife to him.
But I can't get along without some appreciation or some-
thing. With him, it's just work, work, work, and where do
I fit in?"

Around two or three in the morning at Christopher's
End, when all those vice presidents in charge of sales had
crept back to their closets in New Jersey, things got
lively. The hackers would have gone through their mus-
cle-raunch on the dance platform. Then a certain tension
would develop around the bar where Carl was serving
drinks and minding his own business. Customers would
start pleading and cajoling, while Carl protested that he
was paid to serve drinks, not to dance, and damnit, until
they paid him what he deserved, he wasn't going to
dance. More weeping and wailing and gnashing of teeth
would ensue. Carl would finally relent, unzip his body
suit, and step onto the dance platform, as the music
blared.

Carl was a trained dancer, and his nude body could
only cast doubt on the straightness of the Creator. It was
one of the most beautiful things I have ever seen, and he
used it as if it were a Stradivarius. Strong men would
weep and queens collapse in sheer wonder as he moved
in the color of the lights, now red, now green or yellow,
the muscles stretched and pulsing against the strong
angles of his frame.

Linda would watch until she could contain herself no
longer, then strip off all her clothes and join him in a
Dionysian celebration as the audience clapped and
howled. Family nights were never like this in Des Moines.
Unhappily, they're no longer like this in New York,
either.

Walking up Christopher Street on my way home one
evening, I saw a wildly improbable pair of figures coming

toward me. One was a long-haired freak who was wearing a helmet. The other, it seemed certain, was a gorilla. Drawing closer, I decided it must be a person. Still closer, I discovered it was Linda in a fur coat.

Linda was unsteady on her feet and just as unsteady in the eye. But when she finally recognized me, one hand of hers clamped on my arm. "I got to find the motherfucker," she said. "He's got ten downs for me and I got to find him and you got to help." I turned to the freak in the helmet, who only muttered, "You take her for a while," and melted off into the night.

Linda's first stop was Keller's Bar. It has been suggested that this waterfront establishment be preserved by the Landmarks Commission as the first and, at that time, the ultimate sado-masochist gathering place in the city of New York. Linda entered the place as if she owned it, plonked herself at the bar, ordered a double bourbon, and asked the bartender if he'd seen "that motherfucker, Jerry the Creep." Keller's was pure theater in the tradition of Genêt's *The Balcony*. At the bar, and around the edges of the room, were the plumbing supply salesmen, electricians, furniture movers, and parking-lot attendants who were playing the sadists for the evening. They were in black leather caps, dark glasses, black leather jackets with a plethora of chains, studs, and emblems, black leather pants and boots, with heavy key rings hanging from their belts. They lounged around like lethargic tigers, drinking their beer and licking their chops as they observed the center-stage activity around the pool table. There were gathered the chemists, hairdressers, junior accountants, and college students who were playing the masochists for the evening, attired in black plastic jumpsuits, fetchingly unzipped. To watch one of those masochists take a stance with a pool cue was to know the full eloquence of body language, right down to the twitch of the buttocks as the shot was made. The tigers would stir languidly.

Like a good horror movie, Keller's was just real
enough to scare the hell out of me. I could almost hear
the sing of the whip, the rattle of the chains, and the
sobbing cries, all as an obbligato to the heavy beat coming from the jukebox.

"Jerry the Creep" was nowhere around, hadn't been
around, wouldn't be around, and probably didn't exist,
according to the bartender. Linda made a few pungent
remarks about the ancestry of everyone in the place,
belted down the double bourbon, and, mercifully, con-
sented to leave.

As we started up Christopher Street, Linda grew less
and less mobile, and we had to find various resting places
on steps and fire hydrants along the way. In lieu of going
to sleep on the sidewalk, she made it to a hash house,
where I eased her into a booth and she passed out.

The place is an ordinary hash house during the day,
serving truckers, garage men, postal clerks, and others
who work in the area. At night, the place goes into outer
space. By two or three in the morning, there usually isn't
a customer in there who isn't on something, more likely
a bizarre combination of somethings, nodding out,
speeding, tripping, and, in the case of the reactionaries,
just plain drunk.

The night in question was my introduction to the hash
house. On entering, it looked ordinary enough, with
groups clustered in booths and others hunched over the
counter. Only when I looked at the groups closely did I
realize that it was a drug-induced caricature of every
other hash house in the country. People were speaking,
but they weren't talking. They were looking at each
other, but they weren't seeing. Their hands and bodies
moved, but their selves were motionless. At the core was
solitude.

Linda sat across the table from me, her head resting
on the side of the booth, her face sagging, one hand limp

next to an untouched coffee cup. She opened her heavy-lidded eyes for a moment, stared at me from light-years away, and her eyes closed. Slowly her head moved forward and her wig moved back on her head until it rested, incongruously, halfway back on her sleeked-down real hair. Then her head was resting on the table. One hand lay on mine.

It was one of those times of ruminative self-assessment. I had led a long life, been a lot of places, done a lot of things, some of them consequential. Opportunities had been offered me, and I'd turned a lot of them down. I'd done a lot of hunting, not quite knowing what I was hunting for. Peace was hard to come by. Why was it, then, that in these improbable circumstances I felt an unfamiliar calm?

Chapter Three

Cory was a bitch on downs. Such sedatives as Tuinols may have been surcease for him, but they were hell on everybody around him. It was almost as if Cory felt that he was in a stockade and could pitch any kind of brickbat over the wall at the passers-by. But nobody could get at him inside the wall.

If he pulled one of these fantasies on the street, he was likely to get the shit kicked out of him. He'd come back battered, but defiant as ever. Things got complicated, however, when he tried one of his little acts around the house. At first he'd try pitching verbal pebbles over the wall in hopes of hitting Bruce or me on the head. He frequently did. But he wouldn't evoke the fine martial spirit he had hoped for. Bruce was a trained prizefighter, and I outweighed Cory by nearly a hundred pounds. Both of us felt it would quite suffice to tell Cory to shut the hell up. But nobody could tell John Wayne to shut up and get away with it. So . . . escalation to a spat of obscenity, a pounding on the table, or a crash of crockery. All of which tended to make the atmosphere a little tense. Bruce would stare at Cory balefully and leave. I would suggest that Cory leave, and he'd either do so, or he'd go to bed and sleep it off, rising the next morning with an amiable disposition and wondering why everyone was frowning at him.

One night he must have consumed some real depth charges because when he came back to the house he was slow-moving and sloe-eyed. I thought he was ready to pass out. But Cory had no intention of passing out before he'd lived through the defense of the Alamo or the Battle of Little Big Horn or some other damn thing. Bruce was out on the town somewhere. Cory zeroed in for a tête-à-tête with me about everything that was absolutely wrong about absolutely everything. The recital took quite a while, and it got more annoying with each passing moment. It wasn't just a few pebbles, it was an unremitting shower of stones. Now and then I caught Cory peeking through the cracks of his stockade to see how he was doing. He was doing just fine, thank you. I was thoroughly pissed off. Finally for a grand climax he upset the living-room table.

At which point, enter Bruce. Knowing Cory, he took about one-half minute to size up the situation and come on stalking. "Pick up the table, Cory." Bruce's voice was even. Cory, playing John Wayne to Bruce's Geronimo, said, "Fuck you!" Which was unwise. Bruce's muscles tightened. Sensing impending slaughter, I got between them. Which was also unwise. "And fuck you, too!" said Cory to me. "I don't need you to protect me!" Bruce circled, sent out one fist so fast I could barely see it and Cory went reeling to the floor. "Pick up the table, Cory." "Up yours!" said Cory. Bruce went after him with the open hand—whip-cracks of flesh against flesh. "You ready to pick up the table," said Bruce, "or you want some more?"

Cory, crouched on the floor: "I can take whatever you've got, punk!"

Bruce: "I'm tired of your shit, Cory, right up to here!" Another whip-crack.

"Bruce," I said, "that's enough."

Bruce grabbed Cory by the shirt and pulled him to his feet. "Are you going to pick up the table or aren't you?" Bruce stood back, his hands poised.

The stockade had crumbled. The Indians had overrun the compound. The flag was burning and John Wayne was bleeding on a pile of hay.

Cory picked up the table.

"I'm leaving," he said.

"I'm packing my bags and I'm leaving!" said Bruce.

"So we're both leaving!" said Cory.

I said, "Oh."

Bruce started a flurry of activity in the closet, in the bureau, and in the boxes under the bed, pulling out clothing, books, mementos, and God knows what else. He spread his possessions all over the living room. Cory tried to follow suit, but the pounding he'd taken together with the downs had left him too wobbly. I was lying on the bed. He crawled in next to me and lay there, his breathing labored. His lips and eyes were swelling, and he quivered. I held him. He drew me down to him, and I kissed him. "I'm sorry," he said. He didn't say anything more for a long time. Then he got out of the bed and went into the living room, where Bruce was going through all his preparations for leaving. I heard their voices, talking softly, until I went to sleep.

I woke up the next morning to find them in each other's arms, asleep on the couch. But both of them left that day to go their separate ways.

That evening I prowled around the apartment, picking things up, straightening things out, and generally putting the place back into its pre-countercultural condition —call it muted academic, or mildly funky bourgeois. The apartment I had found in the Village suited my style beautifully. It was a floor-through basement in an old renovated Federal-style building a couple of blocks from Sheridan Square. Basically it was one big room with three doors—the front door, the back door into the garden, and the door to the john. Toward the front, one area served as a living room, another as a study, and still another as a kitchen. Toward the back, separated by a curtain, was the bed and dressing-room area and the bath. The place had beamed ceilings, white walls, and, in the living-room area, a large raw-brick fireplace that didn't work and in which I kept candles burning. When I moved in I brought with me a king-sized bed. In the course of the year, this was replaced with a waterbed of about the same size.

The ambiance of the place was eclectic. Parts of it looked like New England Colonial, other parts looked like a professorial study, and still others, with those sandy white walls, looked like my mental image of a whorehouse in Marrakech. At any rate, it was my pad, and I loved it.

But that evening, after Cory and Bruce had left, the apartment had a hollow ring. I tried to shrug off the previous month or so as an incident in the life bohemian, but it wouldn't be shrugged off so easily. After dinner, I sat down and read *Time* magazine cover to cover, but even that narcotic didn't relieve my angst. The life had gone out of the place, the vibrancy was lost, and sweet order had lost its savor.

For the next few days I spoke harshly to checkers at the A&P, argued with good friends, and thought of reading Spengler. If I had had a cat, I would have kicked it.

Failing that, I got drunk and concluded that I was well rid of those crazy freaks and would hereafter devote myself to monastic improvements of the mind.

Fortunately, I was saved from such a fate several days later.

Among the sundry people that Bruce had brought around to the house was a Watusi named Vernon. It would be an overstatement to say that Vernon was nine feet tall. He just looked that big; you could see him standing on the plains of central Africa, resting on a spear and one leg, surveying the horizon for lions.

At least that was the first image of Vernon. After that it got complicated. It kept getting complicated for months and months and, as a matter of fact, it's still pretty complicated.

First of all, there was the matter of Vernon's eyes. They sure as hell didn't belong on the plains of Central Africa. They were out of *The Arabian Nights*, and Vernon knew just how to use them: watchful, baleful, suggestive, seductive, and then a flicker of bemusement.

Then there was the matter of Vernon's voice, a bass that Robeson could have been proud of, but in Vernon's case it purred, and, like a cat, it rubbed against you and left its echoes.

And finally there was the matter of Vernon's pants. They were worn out when I met him. Now, a year later, they are still worn out. In the course of the year they have been sewn together, patched, studded, and, for all I know, lithographed, into a veritable harlequinade of fabric and leather improvisation. Other people might work on a diary, Vernon worked on his pants, and like artists before him, he went through various periods. During the time that he and I were lovers, he was in his leather and silver-stud period. From there, under the influence of a horde of Puerto Ricans, he went into a flowered print period. He's now back on solid colors, like late Matisse. Not that he can't afford a new pair of pants; that's entirely beside the point. Vernon's pants are Vernon's public personality, a statement of self and a smite to the Philistines. What Cory did with chains, bracelets, and earrings, Vernon did with his pants. In both cases, the statements were handwrought. Cory made his own chains, link by link, just as Vernon patched his pants.

Vernon kept drifting around to my apartment every so often to check out the situation. He was a lot of fun, exuding a kind of hearth-fire warmth, punctuated with a low rumble of laughter. He had a head on his shoulders and a range of interests far wider than most gays I had known up until that time.

Three days after the big departure of Cory and Bruce, Vernon showed up at the apartment with a tall willowy young black named Lamont. No explanation was given. As I was later to learn, no explanation was needed. Lamont needed a place to stay and he was being brought over for my inspection. I've never known just how explicit these arrangements are. Did Vernon know that Cory and Bruce had moved out? Did he further know that I was feeling a bit gloomy about it? Vernon had a keen social sense. He would act in a situation like that. But once the interested parties were introduced, it was up to them to work it out.

For openers, I asked Lamont where he was from.

"Ethiopia."

That was a stopper. What did he do?

"I'm a dan . . . cer." The two syllables delicately detached.

Where did he get his training?

"At the Bolshoi in Moscow."

Oh.

"And then the Royal Ballet in London."

Oh.

"And then I came to the United States to study at the Juilliard."

Oh.

"But I got thrown out of Juilliard for slugging a teacher."

It was quite an opener.

But Bolshoi or no Bolshoi, Lamont was one beautiful boy. Someone who had been around that much promised to be interesting, too. When Vernon decided that he had six vital appointments in seven parts of town in the next hour (par for his course), I suggested that Lamont hang around. Lamont murmured, "Thank God."

Four days later, Vernon showed up again to announce that Lamont had disappeared. He had, indeed. He hadn't been out of the house since he had first set foot in it.

There is something about a dancer's body. A straight friend of mine who was spending his life in the performing arts had a penchant for Jewish sopranos. He was a psychic masochist whose orgasms were enhanced by renditions from *Così fan Tutti* and subsequent infusions of chicken soup to keep his strength up. But after matins of scales, and vespers of high temperament, my friend would begin to get gray around the gills, and yearn for a ballerina—young, long of limb, and blessedly reticent. "It's not just that they can do things in bed that nobody else can do," he explained to me clinically, "it's the way they move. It all sort of ripples like a cat." After several weeks of ballerinas, my friend, smiling and content, would return to the wars with sopranos. It was a way of living.

I'd think about my friend as I watched Lamont, stripped to the waist or nude, move around the apartment. In truth, he rippled, and I would think of a Leonardo anatomical sketch, every muscle come to life from the yellowed page.

But Lamont was no reticent and pliant ballerina. The role he played was the Queen of Ethiopia, all regal flamboyance and disdain for the peasantry. He drove the rednecks and straights of the Village—a long-suffering lot—right up the wall. Queens they could take. Blacks they could take. But this black queen was beyond endurance. Lamont knew it, and played them to the hilt, camping it up outrageously in whatever public circumstances would preclude outright counterassault.

All this public role-playing was distinctly weird. I lived with Lamont; I slept with Lamont—and this high-camp performance was not the boy I knew. Inside the house he was mild, dreamy, soft-spoken, with a fey sense of humor. In bed he was gentle, assured, and altogether wonderful. Asleep was about the only time he looked as young as he actually was—seventeen—curled up in a kind of childish contentment with a trace of baby fat still in his cheeks. Then he'd open those eyes, and stare. They were big and brooding and sad and poignant enough to melt the stone men on Mount Rushmore.

Lamont languished, and it annoyed the hell out of me. Here was this kid with dance training coming out of his ears and he wasn't doing a damn thing about it except running up and down Christopher Street, shrieking it up with other queens. On occasion I felt compelled to go into my song-and-dance routine on the Protestant work ethic. Lamont would look at me poignantly and retire to Christopher Street. Whenever he needed money, he'd apparently plug into his grandmother's till for an advance on his inheritance from his father who, he told me, had been a vice president of the Ethiopian airline before he died. Whenever things got depressing, Lamont would threaten to take off for Addis Ababa on one of Daddy's planes, never to return. I was impressed.

Lamont's escape hatch to Addis Ababa was the envy of the other queens with whom he used to hang around. Most of them carried on a precarious existence aided by welfare or unemployment insurance, hustling, dealing, ripoffs, and amiable Johns. The knowledge that one

among them had an airline in the family led to all sorts
of fantasies—like Tangiers and beautiful Arab boys. But
one of the queens expressed a certain caution. "It goes
to Addis Ababa, honey. Addis Ababa . . . are you *ready*
for *that?* And is Addis Ababa ready for *you?*" There followed at least ten seconds of silence. It was worse, if
possible, than contemplating Red Bank, New Jersey.

Lamont's most kindred queens were Ronnie and
Bobby. When the three of them got together, it was like
a scene out of *Macbeth,* with mysterious signs, symbols,
and incantations. Ronnie was a tall, lean Mexican of eighteen who had habitually gone around in drag but who
had recently turned over a new leaf and grown a beard.
Old habits die hard, however, and Ronnie still sported
Turbans, earrings, bracelets, and plunging necklines.
Bobby was Polish, with a head of hair worthy of Harpo
Marx. Bobby liked to encounter disasters, real or imag-
ined, in order to survive them, rather in the manner of
an old Joan Crawford movie. I never saw him in full drag,
but he was heavy on makeup and long gossamer scarves
of various pastels. He had a husky voice, a Bronx accent,
and a superb sense of narrative.

The three of them would gather around the table in
the living room and review the turmoils of their hard life.

Bobby: "So I'm coming up from Danny's and I see this
humpy num-bah. Oh, Miss Thing, he was *hung!* And I
said to myself, honey, I'm going to do his buns. So I
cruise him, and we get rapping, and then he starts giving
me a hard time about how straight he is. So I come on
strong and tell him, I mean, Mary, you'll get *over* it!" A
snap of the fingers and a pound of the knuckles on the
table. "So I took him home, and let me tell you, I did him
for utter filth, you better know it! And he loved every
gleaming minute of it!"

I don't remember how the subject of suicide came up
one evening, but Ronnie and Bobby had plenty to say.

Bobby: "There I was in the ladies' room at the Sanctuary, out of my mind on downs because Jerry [his lover] has been such a fucking troll like you wouldn't believe, telling me he's leaving and all. So I have this razor for cutting hash and I decide, let me tell you, Mary, that I'm really . . . really going to cut hash that night. What I know next is that there's all this blood all over the booth, and it's me, bleeding from both wrists, and I'm screaming. Felicia, that dizzy queen, comes running in, and she looks at me and says you're bleeding. And I say, I know I'm bleeding. Like, I'm dying! The cunt is on some heavy grass and she starts giggling . . . you know, because it's all *red* . . . such a crazy shade of red like the lipstick she always wanted . . . and she starts putting it all over her lips . . . and she looks just like Marilyn Monroe in *Some Like It Hot* . . . and I keep thinking how funny it is, her looking like Marilyn Monroe . . . and she's coal-black . . . and I get giggling . . . and the blood is going all over the floor . . . and I dunno . . . I woke up in this hospital with this groovy doctor standing there . . . and I thought I was in heaven!''

Ronnie liked drowning better. He wanted to turn into seaweed: "You know, the way it moves. I always wanted to move like that, so graceful, so free, just letting everything happen and going with it. And I'm standing on this bridge, looking down and watching the weeds all moving like long hair. The water looked deep and so soft and I could be part of it and I wouldn't have to be part of anything else, not all the shit I was living through. And I jumped. But it was only three feet deep, and mud, and there I was standing up to my hips in the stuff, and these clowns come along on the bridge and ask me what the hell I'm doing. What am I doing? I'm killing myself, that's what I'm doing! And they're laughing at me! They're telling me that's no place to dig for clams. Clams, yet!'' Ronnie and Bobby collapse in gales of laughter.

When Bobby first came around, he was living with

someone he described as "an absolute and utter troll."
The way he went on about it, I had visions of some
snaggle-toothed Uriah Heep type of about seventy who,
for some strange reason, held Bobby's lily-white body
helpless in his wizened thrall. One day we had to go up
to the troll's apartment so that Bobby could pick up
some clothes. What we walked into was a sculptor's studio, dominated by a couple of stands with plaster figures
on them, sacks of plaster, mounds of clay, rolls of wire,
and shoved over in one corner, as an afterthought, a
mattress. Poised at one of the stands was a notably attractive guy in his early twenties wtih long hair, strong fea-
tures, and a lithe, slight body. This was Bobby's "troll."
His name was Claude.

While Bobby was messing around in one of the closets,
I looked over Claude's work. The figures, mostly male
nudes, had a lean Giacometti look. Claude commented
on each figure with a vague detachment. His voice was
deliberate, his accent tinged with British, his manner
abstracted. But once in a while his face lit up with a
gentle smile, and I'd know there was somebody there.

Bobby found what he was looking for. He and Lamont
went out to terrorize Christopher Street, and I stayed
around to talk with Claude. Although he was born in
America, he'd gotten both his art and his sexual education in England, and had eventually fled his lover, who
was "faithless, absolutely faithless," and come back to
America to continue his sculpture. As far as Bobby was
concerned, all Claude could do was shrug: "They come
and they go."

In the next couple of days, Bobby left to take up residence with a local bartender in his forties. So much for
the inexplicabilities of gay taste. Claude was left to his
plaster and his solitudes.

But not for long.

Vernon, who had originally brought Lamont over to

my apartment, had had an apartment of his own in the depths of the East Village. But he got laid off his job, the landlord became restive, and Vernon, soulful-eyed, landed at my apartment.

I delighted in Vernon, but since Lamont was already in residence, things were a bit crowded. Waking up in the morning with Lamont on one side of the bed, and Vernon on the other, I'd stare up at the ceiling and mutter, "Dr. Livingston I presume."

Since Claude, the sculptor, began coming around, and was now in solitude after Bobby's departure, and since I was overly blessed, and since Vernon and Claude had taken a liking to each other, Vernon moved in with Claude, all of which stabilized the situation for a while.

As time went on I became increasingly bemused by the game of musical apartments that was endemic to the scene. Cory, for instance, rarely had had a place of his own as at Bayard Street. He usually kept moving from one gay household to another—a month here, several months there. Sometimes it would be another single male; sometimes a commune; sometimes a multiple dwelling of sheer chaos that defied description.

There was a certain protocol to the making and unmaking of these living arrangements. First the casual visit, then the getting into bed, then the "staying over a few days," then the moving in of clothes and helping out around the house, and finally, as a sign of trust and formal domesticity, the duplicate key. The reverse process was roughly the same. First the going out with friends, then the staying away for a few days, then the turning in of the key, but "keep my clothes for a few days, and I'll be back for them." That might or might not be the end of it. One of the guys who lived with me, having departed a month previous, came back for a visit and I suggested he take his clothes with him when he left. Abashed, he asked, "You're not throwing me out, are you?" I allowed as I thought maybe being gone a month was a fair sign that he was out. I was wrong. He left his clothes and in another week he was back. Cory was another great clothes-leaver, and so was Bruce. Eventually the closet became a kind of clothing exchange. One of Bruce's pair of striped pants went the rounds of four or five other wearers until Bruce finally came back and retrieved them. The attrition of socks was so severe that I finally found a source on Canal Street where I could pick them up at twenty-five cents a pair. Still they went. Others appeared in all fabrics and colors, until finding matching socks became a major project.

The mating habits of gays, as Paul Goodman has pointed out, are highly democratic. A gay who is living with a coterie of addicts on welfare in some far reach of the East Village might move from there to some professional's opulent pad on the Upper West Side. A street freak I knew who was a masochist found heaven-for-two with an industrialist on Park Avenue in the Eighties. "You better know it, he ties me up in *velvet* every night! It's getting so I come just touching velvet!" In the course of time I found myself—shall we say—one handshake away from a most astonishing variety of people, not just in the arts and professions but in business right up to the chairman-of-the-board level. I was also interested to note a considerable lavender streak running through the lower levels of—of all things—the Mafia, an organization I had been led to believe was given to firm hetero domesticity. But members of the Mafia had interests in various gay bars and soda joints around town, and an equally keen interest in some of the customers, who happened also to be guys who hung around my place. So I developed a rather strange interchange with Godfather types. It reached a climax of a sort one summer afternoon when some of my egghead neighbors were assembled outside the house. A long, sleek black Cadillac pulled up in front of the house with two white-on-white types in the front seat. Out of the back seat came one of my Cherished, duly delivered, and the Cadillac purred away. The expression on the neighbors' faces was something to behold.

The gypsies who moved around were generally discreet about their liaisons, and only occasionally would a remark be dropped like Lamont's when we were out for a walk: "Yeah, I used to live in that building over there with a psychiatrist . . . couple of months . . . couldn't stand it any longer . . . he was crazy."

Pairing and unpairing sparked various amounts of emotional voltage. Cory usually made his exits on high C and disappeared in a burst of brimstone. Sometimes I was the one who hit high C, with an outstretched arm and finger pointing to the door and Outer Gehenna: "Goddamnit, *out!*" But most partings were in a lower register with a few idle mutterings and a drift toward the door: "It's been real." Or, "See you around." Or, "I'll be back next week." A promise that no one believed.

Regardless of the degree of emotional voltage that attended the parting, the duration of the charge was remarkably short. New arrangements were made, new alliances formed, and life went on. Each member of the unpaired couple relegated the other to a special stature —"my ex-lover." A queen like Bobby, with his penchant for high tragedy, might imply that he had just spent a few months bedded down with Count Dracula. But such animus seemed rare. In most cases, references to "my ex-lover" were either casual points of authority or time frame, and they were usually made with a touch of nostalgia: "Last summer when Sam, my ex-lover, and I went to Fire Island. . . ." Or, "Sam never could stand carrots, but I like them." It was reminiscent of Somerset Maugham in old age bewailing the fact that nobody could make martinis as had his ex-lover. Compared to the *Sturm und Drang* that not infrequently accompanies breakups of straight couples, the comparative gentleness of gay breakups seemed quite refreshing. Perhaps it is due to the assumption of temporariness in gay relationships, contrasted with the assumption of permanence in straight marriages. For the gay, then, every day in a relationship is net profit against the eventual demise of the relationship. The demise comes as inevitably as death, and with the same sadness. The difference is that the demise is expected. Or is it? I'm not all that sure. Underneath the acceptance of short-lived affairs there is the ghostly ideal of "Mr. Perfect," the ultimate guy. Which brings us back to the emotional content of the gay pairing process.

In my experience, at least, the courtship phase never seems to involve much editorial comment, that verbal foreplay that can be so cherished a part of the preliminaries of straight bonding. Verbally, gays can get very streamlined. For openers, "Your place or mine?" For nosegays and bouquets, "You've got a nice body." And for after-sex summations, "That was far-out." Sparse stuff, this. But to go by the verbal script is to miss the point. Sex itself is the language of choice, and eyes do a lot of talking. Beyond the initial eye-lock when cruising becomes consent, one-night quickies don't seem to involve much more eye-work. Sometimes guilt keeps the eyes from ever meeting again for more than a fleeting moment and there is an earnest concentration on the business at hand, almost as if it were some sublimating activity to keep any real contact from developing. At other times, when the vibes are working right, there's the long searching stare, as if some runic mystery is to be deciphered in the other's retina. Beyond the stare, the physical language of sexuality takes over. If it's more than just a number, the saying goes, you *know*, baby, you *know!*

As often as not, both individuals involved recognize the significance of what is happening, and the realization is likely to scare the hell out of one or both of them: I'm not like that. I'm not ready for this. Or, in the great line from *Boys in the Band,* the "Christ-was-I-drunk-last-night" syndrome. Yet the realization of potential is there, and if one of the individuals involved flees the next morning, never to return, the realization is no less potent; it's just aborted. The memory lingers on, and the wistful wondering that perhaps—if I hadn't lost my nerve —I would have found out that he really was the ultimate guy.

A lot of times, of course, the relationship is not aborted by the impact of that first realization, but goes on to run the gauntlet of disenchantments, adjustments, and compromises all flesh is heir to. "George is heaven in bed, but Christ, I wish he'd learn to put the cap back on the toothpaste tube!" The poignant realization that George may not be the ultimate guy, but he'll do. Curiously, as in the case of straight marriages, the death of romanticism and the terrible realization that George is *never* going to learn to put the cap back on the toothpaste tube can lead to the thought that, warts and all, George is about as close as you're going to get to the ultimate. When pairings like that break up, the wounds can be deep and lasting, and all bets about a gentle parting are off. The wrenchings, anguish, and recriminations would rival the goings-on in any divorce court.

In a sense, then, it is the very coolness and temporality of most gay relationships that keeps gays sane. Easy come, easy go, and nice while you're here. All very existential. Now is now and let's enjoy it. Tomorrow is another day. There's a strange analogue here to Alcoholics Anonymous in the idea of limited commitment. It's not "I'm never going to take a drink again for the rest of my life." It's just "I'm not going to drink *today.*" Once the alcoholic and the gay start thinking about the rest of my life, things get heavy. The beauty part, however, is that every day is today.

I have a feeling that in their adherence to the "today" of a relationship, gays have a greater intuitive under-standing of the nature of human relationships than those straights who are concerned about "the rest of my life." Gays get into trouble when they begin to think like straights and get tangled up in all those tomorrows.

Chapter Four

A Scotchman keeps track of his wallet. I'd check through mine at night to assess the day's economic debacle and what money I didn't have for the morrow. A ten dollar bill was conducive to a good night's sleep. One night, during the month or so that Lamont was around, I went to sleep soundly. The next morning, however, the ten dollar bill I thought I had was gone. The night before I had gotten pretty befogged with alcohol. I figured I had probably had some delusions of economic grandeur at one of the local pubs and blown the ten dollars. So I made my customary solemn resolution to grow up, straighten up, and fly right, and forgot about it.

Lamont had a friend named Michael who was also a dancer—and worked at it. Michael used to come around quite a bit on his way to and from dance class. With Michael on one side, pushing, and me on the other side, shoving, we began to get Lamont stirred up about dancing again. He decided to go to the dance class that Michael attended. To get admitted, Lamont had to make up a professional biography. By the time he got through with it, it was a full single-spaced typewritten page detailing his dance experience from Addis Ababa, through Moscow, to London and New York. The full name he put down was Lamont Courtney Bostwick. I felt sure that he'd be accepted, with a wooden leg, on the name alone. Michael read over the biography and raised an eyebrow. "If Lamont's done half the things he says he's done, he'd be with Balanchine." But he didn't say anything more.

Lamont got accepted at class, probably less because of his claims than because he was a pretty good dancer. With Lamont in residence, Michael in attendance, and a variety of like-talented friends and acquaintances of theirs hovering around, evenings at my place were highly athletic. Various series of "movements" were likely to make havoc with side tables, lamps, and ashtrays, and at the end of the evening the apartment had the ineffable odors of a men's gym. The recitals, exercises, movements astonished friends of mine who were likely to show up unannounced. They didn't know what hit them. When *Swan Lake* was followed by the Stones, the corps de ballet would give the general impression that they were out to cook a missionary.

But the Dionysian choreography that took place at the apartment was a sarabande compared to what went on at the Firehouse. The headquarters of the Gay Activist Alliance was an old firehouse on Wooster Street in SoHo. Dances were held there on Saturday nights as a manifest of "Our Place" as opposed to the Mafia-run gay bars in other parts of the city. For two dollars' admission one could spend an evening immersed in tribal rites, with all the soda or beer one could drink. The street floor of the Firehouse was the dance floor, with a circular staircase to the second-floor lounge and soda bar. The basement in Stygian darkness, included chairs, tables, and another soda bar.

The whole building, on Saturday nights, pulsed with the beat of rock music, but the main action was on the dance floor. When Lamont, Vernon, Michael, and I were going over there, it was early June, 1971, and hot, since the Firehouse didn't have air conditioning. The higher the temperature went, the more clothes came off, down to the briefest of hot pants. The music blasted. The bodies writhed. The sweat poured. And the beat went on. Observing the melee from halfway up the circular staircase left no doubt in my mind about what was happening. It was a war dance. The contrast to the dancing at Christopher's End and other dance bars was obvious. At the bars dancing was, by and large, part of the whole cruising process and had a sense of display about it. People danced for other people to see them and hopefully appreciate what they saw. Although plenty of cruising went on at the Firehouse, the dance floor wasn't the place for peacock displays, but a celebration of post-Stonewall identity. "We are. We are together. And if you don't like it, *fuck off!*"

Lamont and Michael were part of the new breed who came out into this vibrant, assertive atmosphere. They blended into the war dance as if they'd been born to it. But Vernon was in his mid-twenties and had known different days. He'd stand there on the sidelines for a few minutes, shaking his head, and muttering, "My, oh my, I've never seen the like. All the chickens are coming home to roost!" And with a beatific smile, he would plunge into the fray.

One late afterooon Michael appeared at the apartment with fire in his eye. Somebody had run off with his clogs at dance class, and the hearsay was that Lamont had been seen wearing them. So where was Lamont? Since it was nearing dinnertime, I allowed as probably he'd be home soon. Michael was not assuaged. "I'll have his ass, the mother," he said, and sat there fuming. "You believe all that shit he's telling you?"

I shrugged. "Why shouldn't I?"

"Because he's a liar is why."

"Makes a good story."

"The crazy cunt's beginning to believe it himself."

"It happens."

"You'll find out he's just a black boy from Athens, Georgia. And he's dirt-poor folk. He's got this act. Damned if I know how he makes people believe it."

"Maybe they want to believe it."

"That's their problem."

Michael let the matter drop.

A few minutes later Lamont showed up, wearing his regular shoes.

Michael socked it to him. "Where are my clogs? They cost eleven dollars, and somebody saw you with them, and I want them back, now."

Lamont looked convincingly blank. "What clogs?"

"My clogs. That you took."

"I didn't take your clogs."

"You damn well did!"

"So I'm wearing your clogs?"

"No, but you took them."

"Not me. And you'll get over it, Miss Thing."

"If I catch you with them, I'll have your ass."

"You won't catch me with them," said Lamont. Then, after a pause, "Because I didn't take them."

"Do me a favor, Lamont. Just for once, tell the fucking truth!"

Lamont was bland. "I am telling you the truth, Michael."

There the matter rested. Michael bought some new clogs.

But a few days later Vernon got the fire in his eye. Ten dollars disappeared from his wallet while he was taking a shower. The only other people in the apartment were Lamont and myself and, during the course of the shower, Lamont had drifted out the door. He didn't return for hours. By the time he got back, Vernon had departed, duly enraged.

When I socked it to him, Lamont was wounded innocence. What ten dollars? And he went into a long discourse on how Vernon couldn't ever hang onto his money. He almost had me believing him.

The brown-off was a phone call from some Upper East Side John with whom Lamont had apparently whiled away a few idle hours. I told him Lamont wasn't in. The John didn't hang up, but went on with some ramblings that led up to "Maybe I shouldn't tell you this . . ."

"Go ahead. I think I know."

"Well, I'd have been perfectly willing to give him the ten dollars but he said . . . well, he liked me, and he wasn't going to take any money because he wasn't into that bag . . . and the next time I checked my wallet, ten dollars was gone."

When Lamont got home, the shit hit the fan. "Sit down." I said.

Lamont looked at me. Wounded. And sat down.

I ticked them off. My ten dollars. Michael's clogs. Vernon's ten dollars. And the Upper East Side John's ten dollars. "So, okay, if you got your arm up to the elbow in the till of both your grandmother and the Ethiopian Airline, how come you're stealing from people who need their money and who are friends of yours? And if all this Ethiopian stuff is a crock, then who are you? This time I want the truth!"

There was silence. Then: "I didn't steal from anybody."

"Shit!"

"I didn't . . . and I am from Ethiopia . . . and . . ." The tears welled up in his eyes. "I'm going to take a walk."

He came back in a half hour. He sat down on the couch bolt upright. The tears were still in his eyes, and I felt tears in mine. His voice was soft and even almost as if, to tell the truth, he had to recite it.

"My name is Andy Jones, and I was brought up on a farm outside of Athens, Georgia. I had nine brothers and sisters, and we never had much of anything. When I was fourteen, they sent me to live with my grandmother up in Harlem. I started hanging around the Village. I met guys, and they made love to me, and I liked that. They took care of me, too. Sent me to dance school, taught me how to speak right, gave me clothes, gave me money so I could try to make something of myself. They made love to me. I made love to them. That's been how it was. I didn't have nothing of my own. Just them. My grandmother, she helped sometimes. But mostly them. They gave me money. I didn't ask for it. I didn't ever want to ask for it. But sometimes they didn't give me anything, and 'cause I didn't have anything, I took it. I took from you, but it was only ten dollars, and it's been a long time I've been here. I hate to ask anybody."

"What's all this thing about Ethiopia?"

"Who wants a black boy from Georgia?" His voice was barely audible. "So I made it up."

I held him for a very long time, and he held me. I went through some heavy changes. Who wants a black boy from Georgia? I sure as hell did, and a lot more than I wanted some gilded youth from the other side of the world. Somehow, Lamont had come home as Andy Jones, and for all the anguish of our racial separateness, stretched for centuries, we were kindred. "I like Andy Jones just fine," I said.

Almost a year later a group of my friends and I ran into Lamont and a group of his friends at the Seventh Avenue

Danny's.[1] Lamont and I were seated across the table from each other. In a mellow mood, I stretched out my hands and he took them in his. "Someday," I said, "little Andy Jones and I are going to make it."

"Who's Andy Jones?" one of his friends asked.

"I'm Andy Jones," said Andy Jones. "The 'Lamont' thing, I just use that. My real name is Andy Jones, and I'm from Athens, Georgia."[2]

Nobody around the table was particularly surprised or taken aback by this revelation. After all, in pre-liberation days, almost everyone in the gay subculture went by a different identity than that used in contacts with the straight world. I knew Cory as "Cory James," not by his christened name of Paul Mandor. And if the gay identity accumulated some trimmings, like being a native of Ethiopia, so be it. The trimmings added color, just as costume added color.

Since the Stonewall Riots of 1969, however, custom seems to be changing slowly. Last names are not particularly important in casual contacts, but when a last name is used, it is likely to be the same name as appears on the person's driver's license.

Early that summer of 1971 there was a gay boat ride up the Hudson. Claude, Vernon, Lamont, and I decided to go for a respite from the heat and a chance to meet some new people. It was the first such occasion I'd attended, and it was quite an affair. Perhaps five hundred people were on board an old day boat, including a crew who, I'm sure, didn't quite know whether, with all those

[1] There are two "Danny's" gay bars in the Village. The first, usually known as "Old Danny's," is at the corner of Christopher and Greenwich Street, two blocks from the waterfront. The other, known as "Seventh Avenue Danny's" or "Dancing Danny's," is located on Seventh Avenue, a block north of Sheridan Square.

[2] Both "Lamont" and "Michael" are doing pretty well for themselves professionally as this book goes to press. "Lamont" was with The Harkness Ballet. Michael was with Balanchine.

people, the ship was going to sink, float, or fly. The proceedings had an amiable old-world atmosphere that was enhanced by the Victorian decor of the boat. People were sitting around tables with their own bar setups, others were at tête-à-têtes at the railing, and below was the dancing deck with colored lights. I had a feeling I was living through a modernized version of a Renoir; it was entirely too domestic and prosaic a scene to have attracted Toulouse-Lautrec. All that was missing were the picnic baskets, parasols, and women.

We started up the Hudson at dusk, lights flickering, music blaring, a babble of talk and the pulse of the engines. Most of the people on board were in their late teens and twenties, and with the exception of a few flashing queens most of them looked like the people you'd see on subways or buses, indistinguishable in the herds of urban life. I got to thinking about that. There's a difference between Gay Lib and the earlier liberation movements of blacks and women. A black is, after all, visibly black. A woman is visibly a woman. But with few exceptions, a gay can melt into the landscape and emerge from it at his or her discretion. It gives the movement an iceberg quality, and only an investigator like Kinsey could give the general public any idea of its undersurface dimensions.

In *Sexual Behavior in the Human Male*, published in 1948, Kinsey stated that "37 percent of the total male population has at least some overt homosexual experience to the point of orgasm between adolescence and old age. This accounts for nearly two males out of every five one may meet." But perhaps an even more startling finding was that "25 percent of the male population has had more than incidental homosexual experience or reactions for at least three years between the ages of 16 and 55. In terms of averages, one male out of approximately every four has had or will have such distinct and continued homosexual experience."

In 1948 findings like these were, to the general public, blockbusters. But they simply confirmed what a lot of gays knew out of their personal experience, namely, that straights weren't all that straight. What made Kinsey's findings credible was that he presented them with all those charts and graphs that the dominant culture cherishes as "facts." But raw dimensions beg the question of who is who. Only at such assemblages as the boat ride is it possible to get a reasonably accurate overview of who is involved, and the only generalization about appearance is that no generalization is possible. Gays come in all sizes, shapes, ages, and colors.

Nor does there seem to be any generalization that can be made about behavior patterns. I kept wondering just how that boat ride would have differed if those attending had been five hundred straight men of comparable class, economic, and educational background. Playing hunches of imagination, I could see more drunks, more fights, less talk, less intermingling, fewer duets, more groups, and no dancing. Okay, then, what if the boat ride consisted of two hundred and fifty men and an equal number of women? Under those circumstances I really couldn't imagine any particular difference, except perhaps that the gays were more relaxed about their courtship.

What does a capacity to blend like this mean to a liberation movement? It sure hasn't meant much in the past. Merle Miller has pointed out that, when he was on the board of the Civil Liberties Union, he defended every other minority interest . . . except the gays. When I was living in San Francisco, a professed gay ran for City Council and got only five thousand votes, probably quite a few of them from women. But you can't tell me there were only five thousand gays in San Francisco! Then there's the image of the Sixth Avenue March, the second Christopher Street Day parade, that took place in the summer of 1971. Onlookers stood on the sidewalks with

stupefied expressions on their faces, but the mass of four
or five thousand people going up the avenue seemed to
exert a gravitational pull. I saw four or five onlookers
step off the curb and into the march itself. There must
have been a lot of others. What, then, will be the snow-
balling effect of more and more people stepping off the
curb and coming out? Does the sorry record of pre-
Stonewall defense of gay rights give any indication of
what is to come? I sat there and looked at the flow and
swirl of the people around me. They certainly were not
any cadre of revolutionaries in the good gray radical
sense of the 1930s. They were a bunch of people out to
have a good time, and having it. But they had a self-
assurance that I can't imagine existing in such a gathering five years before. If the activities at the bars involved
peacock display, and the dances at the Firehouse were
celebrations of militant identity, the goings-on at the
boat ride were a statement of change achieved, an internal liberation made visible in the casual confidence of
people who know they're on their home turf and, most
important, know that they have a home turf.

The boat passed under the massive darkness of the
George Washington Bridge, turned around, and started
back down the river. I was on the top deck, alone, while
the kids were whooping it up on the dance deck. After
the pack of people, it was good to be alone. The couples
on the top deck kept very much to themselves. I watched
the bridge, and played time games with myself. I could
remember when the bridge was built, remember when I
used to walk back and forth across it, remember seeing
it from the Cloisters, remember the loom of it coming
back from weekends in New Jersey. I was twelve. I was
twenty. I was thirty-two. Things that had happened on
the bridge were checkpoints through the years. Passing
under it was another checkpoint; I'd never done that
before.

The bridge receding in the distance, I went downstairs to the dance deck. Watching Lamont, Vernon, Claude, and a lot of other people I knew out there on the dance floor going through the improbable gyrations of youth, I began to play time games again. Every two minutes a year passed; that was the game. Ten minutes was five years. Twenty minutes ten years. Forty minutes, twenty. What was going to happen to those people on the dance floor as the minutes rolled by? Where would they be? What would they be doing? What would they look like? How would they feel? What would they think about themselves?

Bobby was out there, dancing up a storm, hair and scarf flying, shirt opened to his navel. He wore tight pants that showed off everything God had given him, including a touch of flab around his middle. He was twenty-three, had a high school education, and a large complicated Polish family back in the Bronx with whom he was still in contact. But he had no job, was heavy into downs, and was living with a bartender in his forties in an apartment on Hudson Street.

Ten minutes until Bobby would be twenty-eight. He'd probably still have his good looks, and a John. Cory, after all, was past thirty.

Twenty minutes to thirty-three. He'd be fighting weight and wearing bangs to keep his receding hairline from showing. He might still have a John, but he'd be working at least part time in some gay bar or boutique where he could cruise those beautiful young things of twenty.

A half hour till his thirty-eighth birthday, the day he was fired from his job and knew he'd have to go back to the Bronx and work in his brother-in-law's grocery store. Johns were a thing of the past. Once in a while he could lure a trick to his room at the Hotel Earle, but mostly he spent evenings there alone with the television set and

went over to Riker's after the eleven o'clock news to have
a Coke, check out the scene, and dish the tea with young
queens.

Thirty-one minutes to the grocery store in the Bronx,
with his brother-in-law giving the orders. He had a room
in a very straight neighborhood but every morning he'd
go to the coffee shop on the corner, drink his coffee and
eat his danish while he watched all those high school kids
troop into school across the street.

Tall black Vernon with his multicolored pants was also
out on the dance floor with Lamont doing the Bump, a
dance graphic enough to make the vice squad blush.
Vernon had said once that when he decided to come out,
he knew he'd be lonely the rest of his life. So be it.
Twenty minutes to thirty-four. Probably a reasonably
good job. A roommate, with whom sex has long since
vanished, but they get along. A penchant for cooking and
Puerto Ricans and grand opera and indoor plants. Not
a bad life. Vernon could appeal to people and he'd probably have a continuing supply of Puerto Rican boys who
liked his cooking and his company and were flattered by
his attentions. He'd get along.

Claude, the sculptor, was over by the railing, talking to
some heavy butch type. Claude liked such types to tie
him down and beat him, if his partner knew when to stop.
"I had a sadist last night," he'd say dreamily. "He was so
sweet and kind." And he'd raise his shirt to show his
wounds just like Lyndon Johnson after his operation.
Claude had money from his family. He wouldn't starve.
But God knows what else would happen to him. What if
he found a sadist who didn't know when to stop? Or
made beautiful music with a plainclothesman in the IRT
Christopher Street men's room? Claude gave the general impression of a victim looking for a disaster. One
could only wonder what heavy stud was going to admin-
ister it. Claude's search would grow more reckless, less

discriminating, as time passed and his considerable good looks began to fray around the edges. On the other hand, he was an artist of some talent who took his work seriously. If he kept at it, what effect would that have? Would the spine of his work keep him functional and this side of disaster? Just what kind of a balance of construct and self-destruct would he work out? Would he end up lionized on Fifty-seventh Street, or bleeding to death in some West Street gutter? Or maybe both, plus a tactfully phrased obituary in *The New York Times*.

Near Claude by the railing was an eighteen-year-old named Al. Another dicy situation there. Even in the low light the bruises on his face were visible. He had been in a fight three or four days before outside of Seventh Avenue Danny's. The other guy had to be taken to the hospital. Nothing serious, as it turned out, but what about the next time? Al was very bright and had been valedictorian of his high school class on Long Island. Instead of going on to junior college out there and continuing to live with his family, he had come to New York to be with his own gay kind. His family sent him money once in a while. He worked at odd jobs occasionally. But when there was no money from home or jobs to be had, he stole, sometimes from Johns, at other times by breaking and entering. I had had a set-to with Al earlier that week, hollering at him what he already well knew—that he was right on the yellow brick road to Rikers Island, and beyond that a place like Attica. He'd sat there and nodded, but how could I know whether I was getting through to him or not? Then, as we were getting on the boat that evening, I'd run into him again and he asked where he could get an NYU catalogue. Which way would he go? It was a starkly clear choice. Forget the year or the decade. It was safe to say that within six months he'd be either in college or in prison.

Out of the mass of people on the dance deck, strands of lives reached out in time and place, in anguish or fulfillment or just a quiet gentle drift toward death. Post-Stonewall liberation? What did it mean? How would the people on the dance deck differ in their lives from those quiet gray-haried gay couples who ghosted around the Village and shared their little amusements during genteel evenings at Carr's, a West Village gay bar of antique vintage, or at home with the television set and two toy poodles? They'd had their day, their torments in the city and their ecstasies at Cherry Grove, and now they had found their safe haven in a rent-controlled two-bedroom on Charles Street. They could only deplore those young maniacs at GAA for rocking the boat. Liberation? Forget it. Just look for a safe haven.

The question remains: Will the struggle for liberation make any real difference in the daily lives of gays fifteen years from now? Suppose all the discriminatory laws were repealed, what difference would it make? Better-caliber jobs, for one thing. A lot less secretiveness and susceptibility to blackmail. For what it's worth, a knowledge that the expression of sexual love is not the commission of a crime. And a further knowledge that the landlord won't throw you out because you're gay, but most landlords don't anyway. Not unimportant gains, these, and if achieved they would indicate a public recognition that gays have their rights just like everybody else. But is that the substance of "liberation"? Does a change of law "liberate" a human being, or does the change of law simply reflect a liberation that has already taken place within the human being? A chicken-and-egg speculation like this has a point. I had the feeling that those guys on the boat ride were pretty far along on the road to some kind of interior liberation that did not depend on any legal structure or stricture. Better jobs, more secure housing, greater social acceptance, might provide changes in the quality of future lives in the time game, but the real qualitative change had to, and was, coming from within. A new sense of identity, and out of that identity a capacity to organize, affect, and change.

Underscore "capacity." Only in the degree of fulfillment of capacity can we expect any substantive change. New life-styles, new institutional modes of service, new employment opportunities, and recreational outlets are all within the range of that capacity. The germinal beginnings are visible. But the questions are also there . . . Is the internal liberation strong enough to overcome a cultural weight of centuries that burdens not only gays but the dominant culture as well? Or is the subcultural transmission within the gay generations likely to lead the younger ones to the same quiet safe havens of retreat as their predecessors, with nothing changed but the rhetoric?

The choice.

The minister pointed to the casket and looked at the congregation. "Marshall Crane. Twenty-four. He could have been any one of you." And the people in the congregation sat there looking at the gray box in front of the altar at the Washington Square Methodist Church. Marshall Crane seemed like a curious misnomer. In the gray box was Wanda's body, flesh I had known, and I guess about half the people in the congregation had known. There it was, right up front in the gray box. "It could have been any one of you."

I'd heard about Wanda's death from someone on Christopher Street early one evening and tried to get ahold of Cory, but he wasn't at any of his usual haunts. The story was that he had fallen or been pushed out of the fifteenth floor of a hotel in Brooklyn. Since he had no identification on him, the body had lain unclaimed in the morgue for several days before any of his friends had been able to trace him down. He had no family in evidence, and was ready for Potters' Field.

At five in the morning, there was a knocking at the door. Enter Cory and Linda in tears. They finally had got the word. The three of us sat on the couch with a jug of wine and had the reasonable approximation of an Irish wake.

A day later, at ten in the morning, the funeral was held. Two of Wanda's friends had raised the money in a day and made the arrangements. The congregation gathered on the steps of the church—the tribe in many colors. The talk was subdued. People sat close to each other. In the center of the gathering was the head minister of the church, looking like any and every other Methodist minister in the country, clean-shaven, with close-cropped hair, black suit, white shirt, and tie, and an appropriate ministerial handshake and smile. In that gathering he looked as if he'd been dropped from Mars. Yet the whole group seemed to move around the focus of him as if, under all the surface camp, death called for some kind of reassurance that stretched back to conventional childhoods. He was a strength because he made no surface concession to the culture around him, yet held it in manifest understanding and sympathy.

The hearse pulled up in front of the church, and with it several mortician types with ruddy faces and black suits. They got the body out of the hearse with dispatch, and then faced the gathering on the steps. Everybody blinked. Squaring their shoulders with all-in-a-day's-work determination, they carried the casket up the steps and into the church. The congregation followed.

The service was led by the younger minister in white vestments. The usual hymns and scripture readings were followed not by a eulogy, but simply a talk, as the minister stood beside the casket. He spoke about meaning or nonmeaning in life, contrasting the Christian view of life with existential despair. His implications were clear. In rational terms, the body beside him represented an utterly wasted and meaningless life. Were there other terms in which to weigh this person who was not, this thing that had happened? Christianity, given its belief in the immortality of the soul, could look at a person and an event and give them meaning through the redemptive power of Christ. But were there still other terms? I kept brooding about that, remembering the Irish wake with Linda and Cory. That wake meant something. Did a life have to justify itself by Protestant-approved accomplishment? If so, precisely what accomplishment? Like being the head of Dow Chemical? Or having six children? Or being bathed in the sanctity of choiring angels? Was it so little a thing that Wanda had made a few other people happy in his span of years, and they were there to mourn him?

At the end of the concluding hymn, the minister stood before the congregation. "I know most of you don't believe in what I'm going to ask you to do, nor do I want you to feel that you should do it anyway. But we are going to take communion. Give it whatever meaning you choose. But we are gathered here. And I hope as many of you as can will join us, and come forward to the altar." To a man, the congregation stood up and filed toward the altar. It was the first communion I had taken in twenty-five years.

At the conclusion of the ritual, the congregation filed back to their pews. The minister gave a benediction, then said, "I am now going to move down the center aisle and give each of you on the center aisle the Embrace of Peace. Please pass it on to the one next to you in whatever way you feel." He went down the aisle, giving what I guess you'd call the French General version, though slightly gentler than might be given at St.-Cyr. The variations that followed as the embrace was passed along the pews were considerable, and the process took a bit of time because the embrace kept getting held up.

The organ music started. The casket was wheeled out. The congregation followed out the door, blinking their eyes against the blaze of sunlight. The street, the passers-by, the traffic, seemed quite unreal.

Chapter Five

I had some playwrighting chores to do that summer of
'71, which required spending a month in Stockbridge,
Massachusetts. Lamont gave me a going-away present—
a dose of the clap. I arrived in that serene manifest of old
New England, dripping and burning and mad as a wet
hen. I had decided to set aside my riotous and churlish
ways of the past six months and spend some time in
middle-class artistic gentility reaffirming My Respectable
Heritage, and how did I start off? With the clap. How
could I sit in a rocking chair at the Red Lion Inn, watching Norman Rockwell ride by on his bicycle, when I knew
that I had contracted, under unmentionable circumstances, a loathsome social disease? It was too . . . goddamn . . . much.

I made some discreet inquiries about a doctor, giving
the general impression that I had a very bad back. I was

sent down the main street of town, a broad New England thoroughfare lined with opulent trees and big clapboard houses, to the doctor's office. In the waiting room was a large Norman Rockwell original of a gray-haired doctor with a young kid as a patient. The door to the doctor's office opened, and there was the gray-haired doctor right out of the painting. Oh God, what was I going to tell him? I mean, had he ever *heard* of clap? It turned out he had. I got my needle with dispatch and great skill, and I was on my way. Come to think of it, I've never gotten a bill. I'm going to have to do something about that. One up for Norman Rockwell and Co.

Recovering from the clap, I basked in gentility for a few days, said hello to nice old ladies, discussed intelligent matters with intelligent people, and, as a salute to WASP bohemia, ate in Alice's Restaurant. People actually live like this, I kept telling myself. The sun was shining, the birds were twittering, the streets were clean, and the bank teller even smiled at me. Wow. The euphoria lasted three or four days. The city seemed very far away and I had several mild attacks of girl-watching, tempered by the realization that I was still contagious.

But within a week, I had had it, and then some. On a day off, I retired to my apartment with a bottle of vodka to get away from all those goddamn birds, bees, and flowers . . . and WASPS. The more I drank, the more significance the phone had. I kept looking at it, and finally I said "shi-i-i-t!" and picked it up. Vernon was home. I told him to grab the next bus and get the hell up here. Eight hours later he arrived, all nine gorgeous feet of him, complete with silver boots, patched pants, a studded denim jacket, and a happy grin.

It is comparatively easy, dear reader, to write about turmoils, anguishes, uproars, and conflicts. It's not so easy to write about happiness. It's just there, it goes on, you feel it. But what is there to say about it?

Those three weeks with Vernon up at Stockbridge were when I began to get this gay thing together and to understand, as I never had before, the emotional power of a good gay relationship. By God, I was *happy*. Even when the vocational chores up there got heavy, I could still turn in on a warm interior core of emotional fulfillment.

Now, how 'bout that? What went on? Like Claude, I spend considerable time and effort trying to collect emotional disasters. If I can't find them, I make them. What was this? Happiness? What was this base-line impossibility? This thing that everybody's after, and nobody finds? No, Vernon was not the girl I'm going to marry, nor was he the ultimate guy. But I learned, in those three weeks, just enough to be convinced that gays can make it in a paired relationship just as well as anyone else, and that the relationship can have immense emotional rewards.

We were, for one thing, relatively isolated and in that isolation had a chance to explore a variety of changing roles. At the same time, even though the accommodations were comfortable, the sojourn had the general atmosphere of two males camping out in the hostile wilderness, subject to attack by Indians or little old ladies from the Red Lion Inn. Christopher Street had infiltrated the Berkshires, the forest fastnesses of the dominant culture at play, and the infiltrators had to stick together.

At the same time, there was plenty to do and lots of people around. Tanglewood was booming; so were the Lenox Arts Festival, Jacob's Pillow, schools of various kinds, and heaven knows what else. Something was going on every evening. During the day, while I was doing my chores, Vernon roamed the countryside in the car, exploring darkest Pittsfield and Great Barrington, with gun and camera. He had a great deal of fun astonishing the natives with his silver boots, hot pants last seen at the

Firehouse dances, and an open shirt. Hippies they had
seen, but nothing the likes of this! All he needed was a
lion's mane and a spear, and the alarm would have gone
out for Officer Obie.

But the younger generation was intrigued, and Vernon had his following—particularly evident at Tanglewood concerts. We'd be sitting there on the lawn, getting
mildly stewed on a jug of wine, when Vernon would get
restless. He would rise, like a pillar of jet, and saunter
toward the bushes. Slowly the members of his tribe
would rise, and stalk stealthily away, following Vernon,
until they all disappeared in the underbrush. The cognoscenti knew that Vernon kept a fair supply of joints
hidden in his afro. (One time, he lost one, and we had
to hunt for it. Talk about needles in haystacks . . . !) At
any rate, Vernon and the tribe would soon return, single-
file, to take their places again and hear more Beethoven
that, under the circumstances, sounded *much* better. It
was a mode of music appreciation that had heretofore
been beyond my ken.

But the objective circumstances simply provided a
context, not a substance, for the relationship. What happened, happened between us in the casual interplay of
day-to-day life. It was casual because the expectancies
weren't all that great. I hadn't give any Macedonian
holler to Vernon on the phone because he was the last
gay on earth or because I had undying love for him. He,
in turn, hadn't come up to find his ultimate snug harbor;
as far as he was concerned, I was just having a clap-
induced tiff with Lamont. If that gave him an opportunity
to bask at Tanglewood, so be it. Hence, neither he nor
I was out to prove anything and could let events take
their course. Which they did.

But the return to New York after a month was something else again. The city was much with us and Christopher Street was rife with opportunity. The crunch

started. All the casualness began to tighten up. Something had been created between us; the question was what was going to happen to it.

In any such relationship, straight or gay, one partner usually takes the "let's-get-this-thing-organized" role while the other is for letting the bells of freedom ring. The differences can be small, and changeable, or they can be wide. If the differences get too wide, the partnership splits up. If they are too narrow and too consistent, things can get awfully dull.

In past relationships, usually straight, I'd been an inveterate bell-ringer, and let the other partner tend to the organization. I sort of relied on the other partner not to let things get too far out of hand. If they did, and if I wanted the relationship preserved, I'd drop the bell cord posthaste and start a big derry-do about getting things organized. But that seldom happened and mostly I was free to bang on the bells.

Poetic justice came in the form of Vernon. He could ring those bells loud enough to split the ear. Not through any particular malice, but for the sheer joys of sweet freedom. So there I'd be, running around the house like a hen with hives, trying to keep things organized, while Vernon was out there, somewhere, doing somthing. This would go on for a couple of days, and then I'd say, fuck it, and ring a few bells myself. At which point Vernon would do a comprehensive cleaning of the bathroom and let it generally be known that I was being callow. Ha! Whereupon would follow a tea-dishing session. I would orate about my hard life. Vernon would use those *Arabian Nights* eyes of his. And we'd end up in bed—to start all over again the next day. Come to think of it, one might have called it a gay version of *The Odd Couple*.

Something was wrong.

I woke up one night with a thought to damp the sheets, a convulsive reemergence of my degenerate Upper East

Side past. I shook Vernon awake and announced, "What the gay community needs is an Emily Post!"

"What's this fish you're talking about?"[1]

"Emily Post."

"You going straight or something? Why do you need her?"

"She wrote a book about etiquette."

"Something to do with food?"

"How to set the table."

Vernon sat bolt upright in bed. "You're waking me up at two in the morning to tell me where to put the forks?"

"How to behave. So people *agree* on how to behave."

"Well, I'd say the first rule about how to behave is not to wake people up at two in the morning unless you want sex." He paused. "And even then . . ."

"That's a beginning."

"In the morning!" said Vernon and went back to sleep.

I lay there and thought long dark thoughts. The phrases kept coming back. "Always walk on the curb side when escorting a lady." "Never raise your voice in public." "Always respect other people's property." "Hand-write, do not type, personal letters." "Never be consciously rude to anyone." "Light ladies' cigarettes." And the aphorism I learned from a grande dame of my youth —"Politeness is like an air cushion. There may not be anything in it, but it does ease the bumps."

All the superficial rag-tag-and-bobtail that I had, in principle, if not in practice, long since rejected as the tailings of a dying and mendacious social order were suddenly back on my mental doorstep. Like it or not, the dominant culture had mutually agreed upon modes of dealing between people that, if nothing else, "eased the bumps" and enabled transactions to occur without entanglement in a lot of extraneous rules of the game.

[1]"Fish" is perjorative for a woman.

Nobody had to get into a big hassle about whether red lights meant stop and green lights go. That was established, and one could get on to more substantive problems in human trafficking.

But the Aquarian subculture, of which the gays I knew were certainly a part, had other interests—the search for meaning, relevance, spontaneity, and emotional reality. Who the hell cares what red or green lights mean? They are just conventions to be questioned. Why, and who says? And maybe it would be better if we did it with pulsating purple-tinted lasers. So every time the subject of traffic comes up, they've got to discuss the question of lasers. Heavy. Someone's likely to holler "Define your terms," and it's a fair assumption that nothing will get accomplished after that.

I tried for a definition: Etiquette is a common agreement on superficialities that enables people to go on to more important matters.

Yes, and no. There was more to it than that, some emotional component hidden somewhere in that frazzled word "gentleman." Gentle man.

Another definition came to mind: Etiquette is codified kindness. Yes, but if it's codified, hasn't it lost its emotional meaning in the rigidities of the code? Isn't that what the Aquarian beef is all about—all campy superfluity and no substance? How can you codify kindness, anyway?

Well, damnit, we codify language, don't we? We agree that certain words mean certain things (more or less). We agree on certain rules and modes of grammar (more or less). We communicate through voice sound or written sign (more or less). And receive some kind of message in the process, don't we? Positive messages, negative messages, questions. All sorts of messages. Only insofar we agree on the symbols can we communicate the messages, and receive them.

All right, then, isn't there a language of behavior?

Don't acts mean as much as, if not more, than words? If there is no common agreement on the meaning of the act, then communication is as difficult as if one person were speaking Swahili and the other Polish.

Take a gross example. One evening your newly acquired lover gives you a kiss, hies himself off to the local gay bar, and doesn't come home until four the next afternoon. Message received: Sincerity is just not the new one's strong suit. Or, he likes you but he's on his way out. Or, by dawn you'd better call the Sixth Precinct or the morgue. But the message given may be quite different: Look, I really dig you, but I feel like the fits are coming on, and unless I get out of here for a while, I'm going to blow the whole thing up. Or, I was going to meet my ex-lover for ten minutes to tell him it was all over and come back to you, but one drink led to another, and. . . . Or, this is the way I've always been, and none of my ex-lovers thought it was such a big deal. They were glad to get rid of me every once in a while.

In each case the message given and the message received would make some sort of sense of the behavior, but it's a hit-and-miss type of communication, and, as likely as not, is going to lead to all sorts of uproar. But if behavior is understood within some common context, where communication can flow, uproars can be avoided. At the very least, the uproars can be based on an understanding of the issues involved.

When we were at Stockbridge, Vernon and I had relatively few behavior options in the context of day-to-day living. Breakfast, going to work, coming back to the apartment, dinner, some event in the evening, and bed. Sometimes one or the other of us would be out of sorts, but the routine was there to rely upon, and the behavior patterns could vary only within certain limits. Further, in due recognition of the hostility of the territory, we tended to do things together, without either arrangement or question. The setup had marked similarities to a regular hetero bonding, with all the assumptions that that bonding implies.

Back in the city, however, the territory was friendly, the options almost limitless, and behavior language subject to any number of interpretations, misinterpretations, and total confusions. We had them all. Take, for instance, the matter of eating dinner. Decades of nine-to-five jobs had set my metabolism to be hungry about six-thirty or so, and to want a couple of drinks before dinner. Vernon had worked indeterminate hours at various times in his life, and dinner might be anywhere between six and midnight. Or 6 A.M. to noon, for that matter. So if he hove in at eight or so in the evening, it was no big deal. But I'd be sloshed out of my mind and mean-tempered as a bear. Hostilities would ensue, based on my contention that he didn't care enough to get home for dinner on time, and his contention that I didn't care enough to stay sober till he got there. It didn't matter that we both, in fact, cared a great deal; what mattered was that we both misinterpreted the other's behavior language. As far as I was concerned, he was an irresponsible alley cat. As far as he was concerned, I was a dictatorial old curmudgeon.

Enter etiquette, code, rules of the game, or what you will. Dinner at six-thirty, and if you're not coming, call first. Tyrannical, but simple. It worked fine.

Gradually, out of the chaos certain practices that could only be described as bourgeois began to be accepted by both of us. Like getting the dishes washed; doing the laundry; giving each other a reasonable idea, on going out, when we'd be back; developing a circle of mutual friends; getting to bed at a reasonable hour—all sorts of strange things like that.

For a while, Vernon found this mode of life curiously refreshing. But there were stresses, such as announcing to his friends hanging out at someplace like the Bon Soir that at the merest shank of the evening, around midnight, he was going home to his lover. It then sounded like indentured servitude. There were stresses on my part, too, as when Vernon would take off after dinner for some socializing, leaving me sitting at home with egg on my face.

Then there were the streets . . . and the Puerto Ricans. Vernon let it be known, with stars in his eyes, that I had not truly lived until I had had a beau-u-utifulpuertoricanboy. Since I had first been really brought out by a Chicano in, of all improbable places, Bakersfield, California, I allowed as I had no objection to Latin types. Vernon said he'd bring one over for a threesome. I shrugged.

Several nights later, after an evening spent on business, I came home to find a note on my desk that Vernon had delivered and deposited both himself and a beau-u-utifulpuertoricanboy in bed. Sure enough, there they were, two afros on one pillow. The kid's name, it turned out, was Angel, and while he wasn't exactly out of an Umbrian chapel, he'd do very well. But the evening, to Vernon's chagrin, didn't go as planned. Earlier, stark naked in bed beside Vernon, Angel had announced that he was straight. When I hove into view, he decided he had to go home to Mama. Vernon and I ended up in bed, staring at the ceiling. "Puerto Ricans take time," said Vernon.

With Angel, Vernon took time. With a languid flirtatiousness, Angel very gradually succumbed. It took Vernon nearly a month, and his persistence was worthy of a starfish on an oyster. Other Puerto Ricans came and went, but it became more and more apparent that Vernon's heart was with the Angel. In the course of the month, Vernon got himself a job and left to set up housekeeping with a friend of his in the East Village to be near Angel.

Time went by. I formed another alliance. Vernon would drop by every so often to share news of his wedded bliss with Angel. Then, one night, there was a knock on the door, and Angel walked in. He sat down, sipped on a soda, and smiled, invitingly. Somebody seemed to be getting his signals crossed. Of course, it would have been nice if Angel had turned me on. But he didn't. A half hour later, he left.

The next evening Vernon showed up. He was not his usual happy self. He was, in fact, downright baleful. "I keep trying to get that kid organized," he said, "and he won't organize."

I nodded, sagely.

"And every time I put the pressure on, he goes back to his mother. So what am I going to do about that? Then he comes back. Maybe eleven at night. Hangs around wearing my silver boots, jockey shorts, and a hat. That's all. Hangs around, wagging that beautiful ass of his in front of me, and when I try to get those shorts off, he tells me he's going straight again. So by that time it's one o'clock, and I have to go to work in the morning, he decides we've got to go out for a burger at Blimpy's." A heavy sigh. "That little bastard has never washed a dish in his life. He leaves all his clothes around the place, and when I pick them up, he leaves some more. He never tells me when he's coming. He just comes around. It gets so I wait for him to come around, then he doesn't, and I'm sitting there with egg on my face. Why should I wait for that little punk? Trouble is, I do. When I finally get him into bed, he's the living end, and he tells me he loves me and hangs onto me, and all that. You know what happens then? Well, I'll tell you what happens then. I get calls the next day from friends of mine. 'Hey, you know, Angel was over at my place yesterday. He sure is a cute piece of ass. You still going with him?' That's what they ask me. I know what he's been doing with them. I ask them what time Angel was over there and match it up with what time he left my place, and he goes right from my place to another place, to another place, like he's making doctor's rounds or something. Doesn't he think *I know?* I mean, these are my *friends.* And they're all having him! What am I supposed to say . . . that they shouldn't have him? Or that I'm not going with him anymore? I mean, there is some shit I will not eat!'' He paused, and looked at me sharply. "Who said that? You said that, to me. You were drunk.''

"I think e.e. cummings wrote it—part of a poem.''

"Poem, huh? Anyway, I guess it fits.''

"A lot of occasions.''

"Yeah, I guess it does.'' And for all his anguish, he grinned.

Chapter Six

※

Way back in the late thirties the radio industry in this country suffered an acute embarrassment. Out of the deeps of Harlem came a bouncy number called "Hold Tight," which had an infectious rhythm that was ideal to shag to. (The shag was a pre-jitterbug dance that involved a lot of jumping up and down.) At any rate, "Hold Tight" swept the country and was aired constantly on AM radio in happy response to popular demand. The lyrics of "Hold Tight" were mostly scat, but what words were phonetically understandable didn't seem to make much more sense than the scat—with reference to such things as "seafood" and "chicken and rice."

The reaction of some of the cognoscenti in Harlem to the song's national sweep of popularity must have ranged from the goggle-eyed to the hilarious because "Hold Tight" had come right out of Harlem's gay underground and was, in fact, a musical celebration of cock-sucking.

Radio station managers throughout the country, once the word got around the industry, had their problems. Should they keep on promulgating obscenity by playing it? Or should they pull it off the air, thereby stirring up a lot of questions from enthusiastic teenagers? If it's obscene, what's the dirt? Well. . . . er . . . you see, we didn't understand the language. I mean, we didn't know what "seafood" was! All right, what *is* seafood? Yes . . . of course . . . thanks very much for calling.

Language. Every subculture has its patois, and the more repressed the culture, the more recondite the forms of communication. I guess part of this can be attributed to the verbal faddism of any in-group—and gays are more inventive than most—but part of it seems to be an effort to communicate to another member of the subculture without being understood by straights. Gays in South Africa, for instance, have an ingenious system for substituting women's names for other nouns beginning with the same letter, and their chatter ends up sounding like a roll call in a girls' school. Well, if you're a gay in Africa, I guess you have to do something to keep the Boers out of your hair.

The gays I knew felt no need for any arcane form of communication that was understandable only to the cognoscenti. Aside from various catchwords—such as "troll," "trick," "John," "buns," "the tubs," "the trucks," etc.—they spoke plain English.

Maybe too plain.

Thought shapes language, it is said, and language shapes thought. A word that has proved useful in one context and is then transferred to another can acquire a rather murky ambivalence because behind the new context is the shadow image of the old one. Like a double image on a TV screen, you're never quite sure what you are looking at.

Too many words used by gays are derived from hetero identities and relationships. When they are transferred into a gay context, they develop a double image that tends to obscure thought and distort action. Gays are not straight. The use of straight words in a gay context can lead to a semantic shambles.

Let's say there is a bonding between two men. Partner A tends to be aggressive, loud-spoken, decisive, and has other attributes that are supposed to be associated with the masculine of the species. Partner B is more passive, dependent, softer-spoken, and deferential. In referring to these partners, their friends are likely to speak of Partner A as "he" and Partner B as "she." And Partner B will know it. He may resent it, but beneath the resentment will very probably make some kind of effort to fulfill the role he has been assigned by his friends, to enhance those attributes in himself that he believes are feminine. In other words, to be the "she" of the bonding, and run around yapping his head off like those God-awful women in the *Flintstones.*

Okay, compound the absurdity. Let's say Partner B splits up with Partner A and goes on to form an alliance with Partner C, who is more passive, dependent, and deferential than Partner B. You guessed it. Partner B will now be the "he" of the bonding, and run around bawling his head off like those God-awful men in the *Flintstones.*

But, A, B, and C are all males who have a right to their identity as males, and should not succumb to some silly hetero stereotypes promulgated by a bunch of barren-minded scriptwriters on TV.

Maybe we need a pronoun for the man who generally calls the shots in a gay bonding, and another pronoun for the male who generally follows along, but "he" and "she" are simply too freighted with shadow images to make much semantic sense.

Semantic problems not only crop up in matters of sexual identity, but in relationships as well. In this era of decline of institutional marriage and emergence of a variety of other forms of straight bonding, straights may be expected to have a growing amount of difficulty with "marriage," "open marriage," "group marriage," "living together," and an occasional quick shack-up. What these various arrangements are called tends to affect what they are and the behavior that takes place within them.

But the whole concept of "until-death-do-us-part" institutional marriage, transposed into a gay context, doesn't make all that much sense, regardless of the various forms of "holy union" that have been instituted by various gay churches. Looking at the underlying philosophy of law that structures institutional marriage, two guiding principles seem to apply. The first is the security of the children during their formative years. The second is the economic protection of the wife from a straying husband to whom she has given "the best years of her life."

It is difficult to see how either of these principles apply to gay bonding. Thane Hampten, writing in *Gay*, suggests that perhaps the urge of gays to get involved in something they call "marriage" is to assure "that the poodle won't be born out of wedlock." But even more depressing is the thought that gays want to get involved simply because straights have been struggling with the institution for so damn long—an "anything you can do, I can do better" kind of attitude.

On the other hand, there is a component—call it psychological or emotional—to straight marriage that does have applicability to a lot of gays, and that component is commitment. In effect: For however long, we two are going to build and share a life together in most if not all of our nonworking hours and, in some cases, vocation as well. The commitment is both private and public, mutually agreed to, and based on the assumption that it is going to last an appreciable length of time, years or decades. That commitment in hetero terms is called "marriage." But in gay terms, two guys who have made such a commitment are referred to as "lovers" even though, in a lot of long-term relationships, the fires of sexuality have long since smoldered out. So there we are: "marriage" is too legalistic a word, and "lovers" is too romantic and sexual a word, to describe a serious gay bonding. The existent language does not define the reality.

"Lovers" does, of course, apply to one of those steamy emotionally and sexually oriented liaisons that are endemic to the scene, which usually last a matter of months rather than years and are likely to end up in mutual exhaustion or in some hair-pulling, eye-scratching brawl. The hetero term is probably "an affair."

"One-night stand" is a useful phrase, covering a multitude of amusements, both straight and gay, mostly on the cool side with neither commitment nor emotional involvement. But what about a phenomenon I've noticed that can only be described as repeated one-night stands with the same person—guys who occasionally appear, snuggle in for a night or two, disappear for a week or a month, reappear as cool but as affectionate as ever, stay around a day or so for old times' sake, disappear, and so on? A friend of mine must have had something like this in mind when he referred to another guy as "one of my constants." A pleasantly disengaged form of emotional and sexual companionship. I suppose there are analoges for this in the straight world; I just never found them, nor heard any name for them.

There's another relationship that seems to defy nomenclature, but can be remarkably strong nonetheless. That's the relationship between queens, a bonding between two highly effeminate men that constitutes a protective bulwark against the world. They'll share an apartment, clothes, food, income, and bed, but rarely, if ever, sex. "But, honey, we're *sisters!*" one of them protested to me. "What would we do in bed? Lie there and bump pussy?" I confess, I broke up. But such relationships are serious and have a fierce loyalty about them that harks back to the relationship of those two poor gypsies in *Midnight Cowboy* . But what do we call them? "Friendship" is a pretty diffuse word to apply to such intense bonding.

In sum, then, it seems to me that we in the gay subculture have not yet found the words to describe the reality of distinctively gay life and instead have borrowed words from the straight culture and, in the process, messed up our identification of ourselves. Maybe GAA, like the French Academy, needs to go into the lexicon business!

In the unlikely event that GAA or the Mattachine Society should set up a "What-Are-We-Going-to-Call-It Committee," I'd like to put in my personal protest about the word "gay." I know. It's the word-of-choice. It apparently has a long lineage. Bruce Rodgers, in his intriguing lexicon *The Queens' Vernacular,* puts its origins back in sixteenth-century France. The word itself has a good, hard phonetic sound to it; it fits well in headlines; and it is sure better than faggot or queer. Homosexual is too limited—functional rather than cultural. Homophile is better although a bit recondite. But "gay"? Maybe we can change the accepted meaning of the word, but as it now stands, *The American Heritage Dictionary* defines "gay" as "light-hearted; lively; given to social pleasures." Maybe a definition like this goes over big at The Pines on Fire Island on a Labor Day weekend, but when I hear some guy laying out his struggle with his own identity in sentence after halting sentence, or when I see some other guy stoned on downs after breaking up with his lover, staring at the wall for five minutes before the tears start coming, am I supposed to describe these people as "light-hearted, lively, and given to social pleasures"? As they say in the trade, "Come off it, Mary!" Being "gay" is a serious business and involves a great deal more than "social pleasures."

A good example of this puzzlement about words cropped up in the summer of 1972. Residents of a block on the Upper East Side got very much exercised about the presence of a bar in their midst called the Tambourine. The story was reported in the papers solely through the voices of the residents, who claimed that the place was a hangout for "transvestites, drug-pushers, homosexuals, and general freak-outs," and it really sounded pretty wild.

It didn't sound so wild, however, when one of the tribe would say casually to another, "Hey, you goin' up to the Tambourine tonight?" or when still another would say, "George wants to go up to the Tambourine, tonight. He *likes* it up there."

I realized I was looking at two images. As a faithful reader of *The New York Times,* I was, of course, scandalized by all those dreadful people who had invaded that quiet middle-class block in the east Eighties. On the other hand, those people happened to be my friends, and they really didn't seem so dreadful. In fact, I found them highly congenial. It made me wonder about all those words I read in the *Times* every day.

The words "bandit" and "gunman" are strong stuff. What would happen if you ever met a "bandit" on a dark night? Could you tell him by a fixed mad look in his eyes, or his stalking walk or the suspicious bulges in his clothing? Obviously, somebody called "bandit" or "gunman" must have some special attributes on a scale of heroic evil.

One of the tribe that hung around the Village was a dreamy, gentle, affectionate kid named Sal. He had got-

ten out of prison in New Jersey in the early spring of
1972 and had come to New York. Somebody brought
him to my apartment and he kept coming back. He'd
appear at the door in the middle of the day with a hesitant smile on his face and a promise to keep quiet while
I was working. He'd sit there by the hour and read. It was
pleasant to have him around, and when I took a break,
we'd talk.

He had a fey sense of humor and a roving imagination,
but when he got serious, he got very serious, and the
thing he was most serious about was not going back to
prison. He had been in and out of institutions since the
age of eleven for various minor infractions and truancy
and, at eighteen, he wanted very much to get his head
together "on the outside." But the years of institutional
life had taken their toll and he had a sense of dependency
that wasn't very prevalent among the free spirits who
floated around the Village streets. Sal wanted to be cared
for, and to follow those who'd care for him.

One of those who cared—at least somewhat—was a kid
from Kentucky named Kirk, who was bright, aggressive,
and full of hell. Kirk was somebody Sal could hang in
with and they roamed the Village like Damon and
Pythias, inseparable. But Kirk got more and more nos-
taligic for his Kentuck hollow and wanted to go home to
see his mother and sister. The only problem was that in
his old Kentucky home there was a warrant out for his
arrest for burglary. Kirk figured that problem was solu-
ble; he'd go home in drag with Sal in tow as his "husband." So Kirk hustled up some money and off they went
by bus.

It must have been quite an expedition (Sal at a later
time got all misty-eyed about one night in Wheeling,
West Virginia), and their arrival in the Kentucky hollows
must have been something to behold. Kirk's drag didn't
fool the local constabulary one little bit. The word got

around that he was back, the fuzz pounced, and Kirk was hauled off to jail. Sal was left stranded in the back hills of nowhere while Kirk spread joy among the inmates of the local pokey.

I got a phone call from Kirk's mother, and sent the forty dollars to extricate Sal from the hills. A few days later, he returned, somewhat chastened, with a bad case of trench mouth, but all those memories of Wheeling, West Virginia. A clinic took care of the trench mouth, and I lined him up with job possibilities in Brooklyn, but Sal by this time was a died-in-the-wool Villager and wasn't about to get himself lost in the wilds of Brooklyn after his experience in the wilds of Kentucky. He finally landed a job peddling Italian ices in front of one of the local stores on Seventh Avenue. I'd go by the store on one of my afternoon prowls and find him there, with a cute grin on his face. And did I want lemon or lime? I was partial to lime.

After beating the rap in Kentucky, Kirk returned, and though the relationship had long since crested, they'd tag around together when Sal wasn't working. One time they went up to Times Square and got their pictures taken, both separately and with a few amorous shots together. They brought the pictures back to my apartment. I remember being no little horrified at one shot of Sal's genial blue-eyed baby face: "My God, Sal, you look like a bandit!"

Sal was getting his head together and making enough money to live. He even paid back fifteen of the forty he owed me. He stayed with some queen over in Jersey City for a while, and then moved into a pad on Tenth Street with sundry other members of the tribe. He'd drop by occasionally. One time he appeared with a paper bag filled with twenty dollars' worth of nickels he'd swiped from some vending machine at Coney Island. I was moderately irate. "You want to go back to jail for a lousy twenty dollars' worth of nickels?" He swore it was his last caper.

In early August he showed up one brisk day to get a sweater out of the clothing exchange. He was all tensed up and confided that some big plans were afoot with some guys he knew over at the Tenth Street place. I'd heard big plans before: the two favorites were going to California and robbing a bank. At one time or another, almost every kid I knew was going to do one or the other. Sal was on a rob-a-bank trip, and, no kidding, he and a couple of other guys were really going to do it. He said. I said, uh-huh, and I was leaving on the next rocket to the moon. He said, seriously, and produced a small hand gun. I told him to get that thing the hell out of my sight.

"All right, Sal, what's going to happen if you get caught? I mean, like ten to twenty, huh?"

"They're never going to catch me," he said, and pointed a finger to his temple.

He tried on a couple of sweaters, taking care to find one that fitted well. We exchanged some gossip and we kissed good-bye. I told him, airily, "Be good," assuming that he'd come off his rob-a-bank trip in the next couple of days.

The next time I saw him was in the city morgue.

And the papers were full of "bandit" and "gunman" and that God-awful picture of Sal. They had it all fitted together. Obviously, a guy who looked like that would be the kind of guy who'd rob a bank. Obviously, he had to be gunned down by the FBI, just like Dillinger or Pretty Boy Floyd.

Sal was part of the legendary "Gay Bank Heist" that took place in the dog days of August, 1972, when about all the media had to report on was the renomination of Nixon for President. In the middle of that wasteland of non-news, a couple of gays go out and hold up a bank in Brooklyn, take hostages, and try to skyjack a plane. In comparison to the "dog-bites-man" story from Miami, this "man-bites-dog" story was fully exploited. The papers made a game attempt to fit into "normal" stereotypes people and actions they did not understand. Who the hell ever heard of a "gay Lib type" bank robber? Well, make him look like any old bank robber, and thus preserve the Republic and the stereotypes for which it stands.

Sometimes gays themselves conjure up descriptive terms of vaguely perjorative connotations. A "dinge-freak," for instance, is a white gay who likes blacks. A "snow-queen" is a black gay who likes whites. Like sadists paired with masochists, they can make a happy match. But the contrapuntals of the relationships can get complex. Not just two people but two races, each with its own history, identity, and residual hostilities. Plus the various pressures of being gay in a predominantly straight culture.

One of the most perceptive studies of this relationship was a play called *Bill and William,* written by James Addison and produced at the Playbox in New York during the summer of 1971. Bill is white and, at the beginning of the play, the fem. William is black and, at the beginning, the butch. Bill is obviously fascinated with big black studs, and William plays the role to, shall we say, the hilt. But over the year they live together the modes of the dominant culture begin to infiltrate their relationship. Bill gradually becomes the butch, William the submissive fem. Then Bill, having brought the Big Black Stud to submission, develops a penchant for beau-u-tifulpuertoricanboys, and the relationship breaks up.

Lamont and I saw the play when it first opened, and before word got around about the plot. It was quite an experience, watching all that going on up on the stage. We caused some consternation among the closet queens in the audience by laughing, entirely too knowledgeably, in places where no one else laughed.

I did some meditating about this whole business of dominance, submission, and race. Both Lamont and Vernon were coal-black, and their blackness was not to be ignored. They were both American Negroes, with all the history that that identity implies. One would automatically think that in a gay relationship, somehow, somewhere, racial reality would emerge in a virulent form. But combing back over remembrance, I'll be damned if I can think of when or where. Sure, the superficialities were there in such affectionate nosegays as "get your beautiful black ass the hell over here." Or, when I was having a fit of Calvinist compulsiveness, Vernon might mutter about "once a honky, always a honky." But the racial issue, in language at any rate, was just one dimension of a far larger interplay that was basically gay.

Nor did there seem to be any great distinctiveness in sexual communication. Roles? You name it, they could play it; and shift back and forth with great ease and high skill. If there was any difference at all that could be defined between white-white and white-black gay experiences, it might have something to do with the degree of emotional warmth. Not passion, necessarily, but warmth —a kind of glow that could generate some far-out vibrations. So help me, at times with Vernon I could feel that I was resting in the arms of my big black Mammy and nothing, no way, could ever harm me. I got some feedback from Vernon along that line of speculation from which I have yet to recover. We were dishing the tea to each other one evening about our situation, and what makes gays attracted to each other and what keeps them together. I rambled on with a recital of what I dug about him, and then paused. "I know what I love about you," said I, "but I'll be damned if I know what you see in me." I sort of expected him to extol my Brilliant and Adventuring Mind, or my Razor-sharp Perceptions, or my extraordinary talents in making red cabbage borscht. But no. "What I love about you," said Vernon, "is that you're just a big old lovable teddy bear."

Now what the hell do you say to something like that? For all the wisdom of my anguished years, I should end up as Winnie-the-Pooh? Here I'd thought all along I was Tigger! But if I'd changed in some measure, it was that glow of Vernon's that had brought out the Winnie-the-Pooh in me. That's what I mean about vibes.

One of my closest friends in New York is a dinge-freak of many years standing who, in the course of the year, was having a breakup of monumental proportions with his lover of four years, an attractive young black named Jesse. Craig, my friend, would come over every so often to talk about the latest installment in his turmoils with Jesse.

One afternoon he got into a general speculation about his relationship with blacks. "I don't know . . . they're so much more *there,* so many fewer inhibitions, and an easiness about expressing themselves that I just don't have unless I'm with them." Then, he added darkly, "The problem with Jesse is that he's *white,* and getting whiter all the time."

But another dinge-freak was more somber. "When I sleep with a fem-black, I feel like I've conquered all of Africa—the Africa in myself."

I'm sure there are plenty of blacks who, sleeping with a fem-white, feel that they have conquered all America. But they just weren't the blacks that I knew.

The saga of Craig and Jesse was no simple black-white story, however. The more I learned about it, the less it had to do with race, and the more with those issues endemic to almost any kind of bonding in this society— varying degrees and directions of human development.

Craig and Jesse had picked each other up on a West

Village street at two in the morning, a ploy from which great things sometimes come, but I have never been able to figure out just how it works. Something about a cruising eye-lock followed by some desultory conversation about matches and the possibility of a cup of coffee at Rikers. Craig, who was a magnificent-looking Ivy League type, could carry off these pickups with great aplomb, and under a remarkable variety of circumstances. His greatest feat was eye-locking some number on an express IRT train while he was on a local. They joined forces at the Forty-Second Street stop. At any rate, that eye-lock of Jesse and Craig must have been some doings. Craig was in his late twenties, Jesse in his early twenties. Craig had a highly responsible job; Jesse was just getting going. The symbiosis began in a hurry and Craig and Jesse started living together at Craig's apartment.

Craig helped Jesse get going vocationally, and Jesse got a job, in a different field, that turned out to be at least as significant as the job that Craig held. They had a close and deep relationship that kept growing as both men went about their work. Then, something went drastically wrong with the organization for which Craig worked. And Craig resigned. As time went on, Craig had less and less to do while Jesse had more and more responsibilities in his job. Craig was just not the guy that Jesse had known before, and as Craig stayed home and got deeper into introspective meditations, getting his head together, Jesse was put in the unaccustomed role of, if not dominance, at least cutting-edge activity.

Still, it was Craig's apartment, a lot of Craig's money, the history of Craig's help. Jesse was surrounded, like it or not, by Craig, and as Craig had less and less to occupy his time, more of it was spent on maintaining some kind of dominance over Jesse. At the same time, Craig was increasingly submerged in Jesse's activities, interests, and needs. The situation kept getting heavier and heavier.

The first time I had a chance to get to know Jesse was when Craig brought him over to the house in the spring of 1971. Cory was in residence at the time, and the four of us had something of an encounter. Cory and Jesse lined up on one side; Craig and I on the other. Cory and Jesse understood each other right off the bat. Their common cause was that they were being trammeled upon by Establishment WASPS who held all the cards—namely, Craig and me. Since, at that time, both Cory and Jesse were, in their meek-shall-inherit-the-earth way, doing a good bit of trammeling themselves, Craig and I did not know just how to handle this line of argument. Further, both of us were interested in keeping things together. Hence Cory and Jesse felt free to pursue their attack with gusto. The whole discussion began to sound more and more like the organizing meeting for a Women's Lib cell, with two males in attendance for flagellation purposes. But it was different, because, after all, we were four men in that room, four male egos having it out. No amount of role-playing could obviate that fact. Each of us, with the possible exception of Cory, had vocations that led us in various directions, and none of us was prepared to have anyone else stand in his light. Nobody could assume the traditional wifely role of subordinating his own ego to anyone else's vocational career. Consequently the encounter was a lot tougher than might have been the case if the cast had included two men and two "traditional" wives. But if the cast had included two "liberated" women, I don't know; it might have sounded pretty much the same.

The turmoils, the infidelities, the trial separations, the trips to the psychiatrist, the split vacations, the all-night soul sessions, and the general anguish that ensued between Craig and Jesse would all sound devastatingly familiar to any marriage counselor who was advising two vocationally active partners. It certainly sounded familiar to me, and the echoes of my own turmoils in the straight world kept beating on my brain. God, is there no hope?

I heard most of it from Craig' s point of view, with only occasional passing comments from Jesse. But the general outlines were clear enough. Two men, who loved each other deeply, were growing at different rates and in different directions of development. The traditional roles that they had played out in their relationship up to now just didn't fit the new realities. The tragedy was that they couldn't find new roles to play that had as satisfactory a fit as the old ones. Jesse just could not admire his currently meditative and introspective partner as the super-energetic power-shaking Establishment type from whom he had drawn strength, confidence, and know-how in the previous years of their relationship. He just wasn't all that interested in shacking up with a swami, and most particularly a possessive swami. He wanted the paternal, not the maternal, and he wasn't about to change his tastes—except in one way. As he matured, he began to want to assume the paternal role himself and his taste in one-night stands gravitated toward kids who were younger, less educated than he was, and more submissive. As often as not, they were Puerto Rican. Like Vernon, he was ready for a new scene.

Craig, on the other hand, was accustomed to running the show, and if the show he favored at the time happened to be an exploration of inner space and a series of Zen revelations, he expected Jesse to play along as faithfully as he had in the various other projects and interests with which Craig had been involved in the past. Craig was delighted that Jesse had gotten himself vocationally near the top of his particular heap, but he couldn't quite get used to the idea that being near the top of the heap was a very absorbing business for Jesse, and that it gave Jesse a whole new concept of himself as a free and self-assured entity. Jesse just wouldn't act the way he always had acted, and Craig couldn't get used to his new way of acting.

They could not make that transposition of roles that had worked—at least for a time—in the play *Bill and William*. Hence, with one wrenching after another, the split-up came. And wrenchings they were. One afternoon Craig came around to my apartment, looking as tidy and well organized as usual. "I just want to sit here for a while," he said. "I just got out of the subway. I was standing there, on the platform, watching the train come in fast. So easy, just to step off the platform. . . . I'll be all right. But I thought I ought to come here for a while."

What could I say? Like . . . "Oh, for Chrissakes, Craig, the kid's growing up. Leave him alone." Or . . . "Go on out to the Morton Street Pier and find yourself a number." Or . . . "Why don't you go straight and find out how different it is?" The last thing he needed was any wiseacre sense from me.

He talked: "I've got to get myself back. It's all been Jesse. I don't know what to think about a movie anymore, or a book; it's what Jesse thinks. If he doesn't like it, I don't like it. That's crazy. But it's happened. Now he's gone away for a while, and I've got to get myself out of this bag. I try. I go along . . . five, ten minutes, sometimes even a half-hour or an hour, and then it hits me. He's not around and I feel this panic thing inside me and that's when I head for the gym at the Y, or take a walk, or do anything, just to be able to say to myself, I am, and I did, and I exist.

"Nights are the worst. I go out for dinner. I come home, listen to music, do some work at my desk, have some friends over or go and see them. Anything. But comes ten or eleven, I'm down at Danny's. I know what happens then. Why do I still go? It's happened three or four times already. I'm down there in the lower room and I pick up some guy, some beautiful guy that anybody would like to go to bed with. I say to myself, this is the way I'm going to get Jesse out of my system, and I take him home. It's not that I can't get it up. I *shrivel*. I'm

standing there. He's standing there, ready to go. And I'm
not going anywhere. I tell him about Jesse, my hangups,
all that, tell him I'm sorry, that if he leaves, it's okay with
me. But he doesn't leave. He stays. I hold him. He holds
me. In the morning we have coffee. That's it. How can
I go on picking up people like that? If you go home with
a guy, you expect some action. But there I am, thinking
about Jesse. No way. But I bet I'll be down at Danny's
tonight. What should I do, put on a sandwich board
saying 'Stay Away'? At least they hold me."

Later I met a few of Craig's numbers. They were all
lean, young, handsome—and black. They glowed, just as
Vernon glowed. They'd pull Craig through, provided
they didn't get distracted with Puerto Ricans.

And Puerto Ricans were, indeed, distracting, as I was
to find out. While Vernon was in residence, he once
showed up with a beau-u-u-tifulpuertoricanboy named
Juan. Vernon's heart belonged to Angel at that time, and
Juan was, to him, a kind of social diversion for the afternoon. Juan looked at me out of the deep dark pools of
his eyes and evidently decided that I was going to be his
diversion for some time to come. I didn't have much to
say about it. After scrutinizing Juan, I concluded that I
didn't want to have anything to say about it, even if I had
the opportunity. Yes, he was beautiful. But there was
more. In contrast to the relatively sedate, even bashful
behavior of most young gays who circulated through the
place, Juan took over whenever he came. He tinkered
with the hi-fi set, the TV set, and the toaster, all of which
were chronically in need of repair. He never made any
of them work any better, but he did make a convincing-
looking mess, which he would then assiduously clean up
before he went on to rearrange the furniture. He would
then invade the kitchen and go through some more rear-
rangements while consuming a Dagwood sandwich of his
own invention and epic proportions. He would then try

on two or three pairs of shoes and two or three pairs of pants out of the clothing exchange, just on general principle. (He left more than he ever took.) All during these multifarious activities he would be telling of his latest exploits joyriding in stolen cars, swiping credit cards (which he didn't use), being chased by cops, skirmishes between various gangs, run-ins with local dope dealers (he didn't use dope), and other such narratives, all recited like a sweet angelic litany.

At which point he would decide that he was horny.

Other people might come in. They might hang around for hours. They might or might not be horny, but as far as any observable signs were concerned, they might just be interested in reading *Time* magazine. Not Juan. With Juan, you *knew*. And you had better pay it mind.

His favorite approach was Theda-Bara-on-a-Turkish-divan, which he could do well, solo, but even better if I were on the couch. The way he could move from one end of the couch until he was on my lap at the other end of the couch was a small miracle of inconspicuous body movement. And there he was, and there I was, and neither of us would be horny again for a while. It would take me a day or so to recover; it probably took Juan an hour and a half.

It was a lot of fun if you didn't take it seriously, knowing full well that Juan would be with someone else by six in the evening. In fact, it was so much fun that I could well imagine Vernon taking it seriously with Angel, and reaping the consequences.

Even Craig, devoted dinge-freak that he was, would make exceptions of Puerto Ricans, and hie himself down to Old San Juan for a week, to return sated and swooning with sheer exhaustion. "Just watching them on the beaches . . . just watching," he'd say dreamily, and I knew damn well that he did a lot more than watch.

What was it about kids like Juan and Angel? Call it, I

guess, the joy of physicality and the celebration of the moment—the loud and clear *Ole!* That celebrant sense hasn't been such a prevalent characteristic of the gay culture I've known. Maybe it is lingering past guilts that keep gay sexual language relatively muted. But if so, why are an Angel or a Juan exempt from the general malaise? Or are we talking about the expressiveness of the Mediterranean culture in contrast to the less outgoing habits of people with northern European ancestry? There is ample opportunity in speculations like this to get involved in a lot of meaningless generalities. Still, there *was* something different about those kids, a sense of joy that harked back to girls I had known who unabashedly and heartily loved sex, not the partner so much as the act itself. Nor did the satisfaction of the act depend on esoteric acrobatics or exquisite prolongations. A good ten minutes in the straight missionary position was quite enough to warm the soul.

Juan had that soul-warming quality. Why did so few others? There was no lack of need, or enthusiasm, or skill, or, in some cases, real love. But joy? Hard to find. Maybe the truest liberation is going to be in finding it.

Chapter Seven

One midnight, after an evening at the movies, early in my sojourn in New York, I wandered into an inconspicuous restaurant to have a hamburger and a cup of coffee. What I found was, at the time, one of the most celebrated chicken roosts[1] in the city of New York—the Stable Inn.

The place was dark, commodious, and had a neighborhood pub feel about it. Social activities centered around the pool table and the counter. Booths and tables were located around the sides of the room in the gloaming. Music from the jukebox was nowhere near as loud as at such dance bars as Christopher's End. The predominant sound was talk, all the way from mutters to shrieks. I gave

[1] A chicken, in gay parlance, is an adolescent male gay. A chicken roost is a hangout, soda joint or what you will, for young gays that does not serve liquor and usually stays open until improbable hours of the morning. A chicken hawk is a post-adolescent gay who likes chickens.

my order to a snappish black-haired young queen behind
the counter and sat there on a stool observing the action.

With the exception of a few young queens, the kids at
the Stable Inn had yet to learn the preening actions
characteristic of the clientele of other gay bars. They
moved either with a boyish trudge or a machismo strut,
and for the most part acted self-consciously virile. They
played hard-driving if not very accurate pool, and when
watching others play pool, slouched, James Dean fashion, with their hands in their jeans pockets, impassive
expressions on their faces. I had a feeling that they were
in training to hit the sadist route at Kellers, the waterfront S/M bar, in five years or so. I was wrong.

"See that kid over there in the red shirt?" The voice
was close to my ear. "I want him so much I can taste it."

I turned to see a handsome thin-faced tense guy in his
mid-twenties on the seat next to mine. "Well, why don't
you go get him?" I asked. "Looks like he's waiting."

"Seen him three weekends straight now. Look at those
buns. Those shoulders. The way he moves. How he's
hung. I think about something like that and I go crazy."

"Well, what are you waiting for? All you got to do is
cross the room."

"No, no, you don't understand. I mean, there was like
this chicken I saw walking down the street in Trenton
and I followed him for five blocks, just watching how he
walked, the roll of his ass . . . till I had to stop in this shoe
store and get some shoes, you know, desert boots? They
had them in light suede, or whatever it is, but I wanted
them in dark to go with my pants."

I kept wondering, how the hell did we get to a shoe
store in Trenton? But I hadn't heard anything yet.

"I mean, that kid in the red shirt, how am I going to
take him all the way back to Jersey? The Holland Tunnel,
you know, it bugs me. All the lights and the cars make
a roar in my ears. Been that way ever since I was a kid

and we'd come through the Holland Tunnel going to visit my aunt in Brooklyn. She had these weird plants that looked like they were going to take over the whole apartment, and one day we'd come in and find Aunt Hester strangled, lying there on the floor with the plants all over her. You like these boots, huh? These are the ones I got in Trenton when I was cruising that guy, you know, the one that looks like the kid in the red shirt over there? Three weekends, every Saturday night, I'm seeing that guy. He doesn't see me. When you're chicken hawk, don't let them see you. You just swoop, right down, and grab 'em with your talons and carry them home to bed. Ever watch a hawk? I did, out in a farm in Ohio I used to go summers. That's where I got measles. Somebody gave them to me and I had it all over, even between my toes. Ever have measles? Wonder if that kid in the red shirt ever had measles. Can't you see him, lying there in the bed, all measley, temp and respiration up, and the flush in his face. Yeah, he's too pale, but with a good case of measles. . . ."

What I was hearing, and what, in fair representation, you have been reading, is the monologue of a speed freak. It was a fairly unnerving experience, the more so because it went on for three solid hours.

The guy's name was Spencer. He was a male nurse at a hospital someplace in Jersey and evidently had access to all the speed he could handle, which was considerable. Weekends he would load himself up with a supply, head for the Stable Inn or another soda joint in town and surround himself with chickens. There was only one slight drawback to these weekends: speed not only made Spencer talkative, it made him impotent. All he could do was sit there, and look, and then go back to Jersey.

The Stable Inn had a natural attraction for Bruce, the boxer who used my apartment as a base of operations while Cory was in residence. If Bruce couldn't be found at Chrisopher's End or with his bevy of black drag queens, the chances are he would be at the Stable Inn, being lionized by the chicken-queens. Bruce's butch charms were, apparently, quite irresistible to them and, being a friendly soul, he would keep trooping them over to my apartment. About all it took was a week or so for the word to get around that the apartment was friendly territory, and the Stable Inn gays that flocked here thereafter numbered as the birds of the air.

At first impression, the attraction of the place seemed to be soda, spaghetti, and sleep, all of which they consumed in notable quantities. Although the neighborhood was a hotbed of drug trafficking, and kids might show up in various stages of high, or down, or tripping, I saw drugs in the apartment only once or twice, and their presence led to some very fast exits. The apartment seemed to be a kind of refuge against the outer chaos, and the clutching of an orange soda can was an affirmation of reality.

The outer chaos was considerable. When I first moved in, a soda joint called the Haven was in full operation in the neighborhood as probably the largest downtown retail distribution center for every known variety of drugs. Sunday mornings, going out to get the paper at nine or ten o'clock, I'd see the flotsam and jetsam of the night before strewn around Sheridan Square and West Fourth Street, kids barely able to walk, kids draped over fenders or nodding out in doorways, blank, lost looks on their faces. I had a sunlit vision of hell.

Fights were strange little episodes that came less from any coherent *casus belli* than from a clash of private fantasies right out of various late-show movies, induced by downs, speed, or acid. Superman would assert his primacy over Tarzan, who'd call on Frankenstein's monster for help, and the struggle would bloody the street. These late-show fantasies were not only associated with conflict, but a wide spectrum of behavior. The queens seemed to have a particular penchant for Diana Ross, Marilyn Monroe, and a bevy of stars from the thirties. Around the Stable Inn it was easy to spot the John Waynes, the James Deans, the Gary Coopers.

One of my particular favorites of the Stable Inn crowd was a kid named Fred who had blond curly hair, an infectious smile, and a clutter of fantasies that would boggle the mind. His psyche seethed with rebellion against cops and all other forms of authority. His preoccupations were with the physical forms of power—guns, knives, brass knuckles, or what you will—that might stave off that authority. He had gleeful ways of discomforting it, like the time he let 125 head of cattle out of their pasture in his home town in Pennsylvania.

Every facet of his conversation reflected one projected image: I'm a man, and I'm tough, and nobody better mess with me. Furthermore, I'm straight, man, straight, and I like to fuck girls.

Yet he kept coming around, and usually in the company of a kid I'd know was gay.

It was, of course, a classic syndrome of the closet chicken, but like Lamont's African prince fantasies, Fred projected his with such conviction that I could almost believe him. There was always the unlikely possibility that he was what he said he was.

One evening he showed up, late and alone. He could barely stagger into the room, and stood there, staring at me through heavy-lidded, unfocused eyes. I assumed it was downs, a lot of downs. I steered him across the room and got him into bed, where I'd been watching television, so I could keep track of him. His pulse was strange, his breathing light, his skin clammy, and once he hit the pillow, he seemed to pass out, eyes closed and mouth open. I kept a hand on his pulse and went on watching the news program.

Suddenly he reared up, swung against me, and his arms held on, hard. His body was soft. His head was on my shoulder, close in. His breathing grew deeper. Together, like that, we went to sleep.

The next day he was acting as tough—and straight— as ever.

But his macho life in the outer chaos began to tell. He developed a cough he couldn't seem to shake. From taking speed, he developed sores that wouldn't heal. And in his drive to assert his manhood, he made enemies —heavy, mob-connected ones. All the fantasies of knives and guns to ward off the evil spirits wouldn't prevail much against them.

He showed up one afternoon. He wasn't his usual aggressive self, but his cover was still so good that it took me quite a while to realize that Fred was scared out of his wits. I suggested he go back home for a while. He figured maybe he should, but he didn't move. The chaos outside the door was, to him, a palpable thing with eyes, a hand, and a gun; the fantasies had gotten out of control.

I walked him to the subway station and we rode the train to the Port Authority Bus Station. On the train, he sat close in. I bought his ticket and put him on the bus to Allentown. Only when he got on the bus did he smile. Huck Finn had gotten out of another scrape.

It would be pleasant to say the story ends there, but the truth's too serious for that. Fred went home, had a fight with his father, robbed a store, assaulted a cop, got put into a youth home, escaped from the youth home, and showed up again on my doorstep within six weeks. At least he didn't have the cough any more, and the sores had healed. But he went right back to the street-and-soda-joint life he'd left, noisy and tough and "straight" as ever.

The pattern of Fred kept repeating itself with infinite

variations until, around the apartment, the slogan "Look, I'm straight, man, straight" equaled "I just do it for the money" as a source of hilarity, at least for those young gays who'd gone through their identity crises. For the declaimers, it was anything but funny. "Whaddaya mean? I *am* straight! Just because I go to bed with a guy once in a while doesn't mean I'm not straight." And, as a clincher, "I just let them do it, I don't do anything!" An assertion usually made with the devout conviction of a Vestal Virgin.

But what is this identity crisis, this watershed divide? As time went on, and the young gays I knew went through their transformations and turmoils, I began to see that the process is a lot more complicated than just standing in front of the mirror one morning and announcing to oneself "I am gay." Rather it seemed to be a gradual process of internal liberation that stretched through the late teens and into the twenties. I could see kids at each stage of the process and, in the course of a year or so, move from one stage to another.

Instead of doing a paste-pot composite of all the scraps and shards of insight I got into this liberation process, perhaps it would be clearer to take one character and follow him through experiences that might lead him to become a functional, reasonably well-adjusted homosexual. We'll call him Billy.

Foregoing all that stuff about "the dominant mother and the weak and/or absent father," let's just say that Billy had parents and a low level of androgens and let it go at that. Assume the usual childhood explorations and the bewilderments of early adolescence and gonadal stirrings, soft-focusing on peers—boys and girls alike. Then, through either experience or imagination, private acknowledgment of difference—very private, barely acknowledged, hopefully forgotten. But there.

At sixteen, Billy clung to the fact that he had made it

with a girl. In the dunes behind the beach. That proved he was okay, and all the other things that had happened, well, that was how it had been, but not how it was going to be. He'd grow up and get married like everybody else, and have children of his own, and he'd never, never let anybody know the other things that had happened.

Billy and his friend Spunk lived in the outer reaches of Queens. Spunk was a little older, more adventurous, and, because his parents were having trouble, he liked to get out of the house and roam. One day he met Billy and told him about his discovery. He'd heard it from another guy, and he'd gone there, and it had happened and it was true, what the other guy had said. It was really something!

What Spunk had discovered was Central Park West, the park side of the street between Seventy-second and Seventy-ninth streets, which, according to tradition, has been a gay pickup area for more than a century. When Spunk was picked up by Rodney, he crossed the threshold into the gay subculture. Spunk in turn took Billy across the line.

All Spunk had, when he came back from that evening on Central Park West, were Rodney's name and phone number on a slip of paper. Both Spunk and Billy would accumulate a whole confetti-load of those slips of paper in the next few years—the coinage of the subculture—tucked away in the back pockets of jeans, folded, crumpled, tattered, and at last forgotten and lost. The big guy with red hair. The cool cat in the Mercedes. The fellow I bumped into on Fifty-eighth Street. That creep at Old Danny's. The old one who spent forty dollars on me at the Round Table and wanted me to beat him . . . on and on. Slip after slip of paper.

Rodney was Spunk's first slip, and he showed it to Billy as if he held Aladdin's Lamp. "You should see this guy's place. Apartment building with a doorman all dressed up. And you go up in the elevator, way up. His pad, it's got a big living room and it looks out over the Park, with rugs all over, and this big stereo, and a bar with all kinds of bottles, and a color television set in the bedroom. He's in some kind of thing down on Wall Street. He's old, maybe even thirty, and he's got it all together. He says like he's bisexual, you know, and he likes guys and girls both. He gave me a drink. Then we smoked some grass and played a lot of his records—he's big on Dionne Warwick—and he told me I had a nice body. After a while I was feeling real good and he let me take a shower. It was one of those crazy showers where the water comes out all around you, and being stoned, I felt like I was all alive —everything—and then we went into the bedroom to watch television, and he talked to me. I never had anybody talk to me like that, I mean, him being older, but talking to me just like I was, you know, his friend. Then he put his arms around me, and I was going to tell him I was straight, but he said he liked girls too, so it didn't matter, and . . . after a while, I came back home."

Heady stuff for a couple of kids from Queens.

Spunk allowed Billy to persuade him to take him next time he went to see Rodney, and Rodney had a friend over for the occasion. The friend made it with Spunk. Rodney made it with Billy, and Billy was in the scene.

The scene, for Billy, was one great big ego trip. At home, he was a kid like any other. But when he was at Rodney's, with the low lights, and the music, and the grass, and the sweep of the city through the window, it was like he was on *The Late Show* and Rodney was Robert Taylor and Billy was . . . ? Billy caught himself thinking "Margaret Sullavan" and quickly suppressed the idea. He wasn't any woman; he was Rodney's friend, kid brother . . . something. He'd go into long fantasies about how he and Rodney were going to take a long trip together to some place like Brazil. They'd work on a project together, building a road through the jungle. Rodney would be the boss, Billy would help, and it would just be the two of them and thousands of natives and a lot of big equipment, heading for the Andes. Billy would have Rodney all to himself. That's how he wanted it. Sure, there'd be women around, and they'd each have them, because they were both straight. But they'd have each other, too, and that was more important.

Billy spent more and more time either with Rodney or in his fantasy world. His parents were vaguely conscious that Billy was going through changes, and that he was likely to disappear for long stretches of the evening, but Billy had always been a restless, imaginative, solitary type, so they shrugged off this latest phase of his development.

But, inside Billy's head, his ego was flowering like a field of tulips. Rodney, he felt, was the greatest thing that had ever happened to him; he was growing up to be a man and Rodney was there to help him. It would go on like this for years and years. . . .

Until that night, a month later, on tequila. All the flattery, all the ego-inflation that Rodney had given him regurgitated. Billy was beginning to believe it himself, and he let Rodney know that he—Billy—was the greatest, and Rodney was mighty lucky to have him around, and that if Rodney didn't treat him right, lots of other Johns were out there, just waiting, to give him an allowance, a car, a dog, a charge card for clothes, a trip to Puerto Rico. But Billy, out of the goodness of his heart, was staying with Rodney, as long as Rodney treated him right.

Rodney just sat there and listened.

Thursday evening Rodney had a business meeting. Saturday evening he was out of town. Monday evening he had some friends visiting from out of town. Billy kept calling, but Rodney always had something going. Finally

Billy stopped calling. He found himself a girl and started dating her.

But after Rodney, the girl was pretty tepid stuff, talking on and on about doing the dishes and what her sister said and when they were going to Jones Beach and what she was going to wear on Saturday night. All the while, he was trying to make her and not succeeding. His ego wilted. No late-show scenes. No upper Amazon. None of that surge of importance that he had felt when he was with Rodney. And—he would barely admit to himself— he missed Rodney's body, its angularities, its strength, and the security he felt when Rodney was next to him.

He ended up one evening sitting on the wall of Central Park at Seventy-fifth Street and Central Park West, wait- ing for Rodney, for anybody. The anybodys drifted by, paused, asked for a match, offered a cigarette, com- mented on the weather, told him how good-looking he was. He could feel his ego stir again. When they asked him to go home with them, he went, and hoped each place would have a big window overlooking the park. But none of them did. And not one of the anybodys was Rodney.

What Billy went through for the next year or so was a corrosive, retrograde process. What had been genuine with Rodney became counterfeit with each new trick. The patterned behavior had a callow monotony, with Billy cultivating a hooded butch insouciance that pre- cluded almost all but the most rudimentary communica- tion. The act seemed to stimulate many of the Johns and they would lavish attention and flattery on him that was as false as his own act. In bed, he just lay there and let them do their thing. Sometimes they gave him money, and he took it. Sometimes they gave him gifts, and he took those, not because he felt any great desire for either money or gifts, but because it was tangible evidence that they dug him, and he liked that. He had nothing to give, but he took anyway. After all, he was straight and they were just crazy faggots. That made it all right.

With one or two out of dozens, he felt a twinge of what he had felt with Rodney. He'd want to hold, and be held, reach out and find someone there. But that wasn't part of the act. Catching himself reaching out, he'd pull back, relax, and let what was going to happen happen without any response on his part. That was the way to do it.

He learned that from his peers, the kids he met on the wall at the park, on the streets, in the lunch rooms around Broadway and Seventy-second, and at the chicken roosts. They'd get together and compare notes, experience, prices, and even individual Johns that two or more of them might have had. The note comparing had the general atmosphere of a union meeting, workers figuring out how to get the maximum benefits for minimum productivity.

In sum, the bag that Billy had gotten himself into had about as much to do with genuine homosexuality as it did with freight-handling. All Billy's needs, desires and urges that had surfaced with Rodney were repressed. Rodney's pulling away had hurt him more than he cared to admit to himself, and he wasn't about to let it happen again. Consequently, the act. It shielded him from emotional hurt, and at the same time, staved off the need to confront his own gayness. He was "straight, man, straight."

The moorings he had to his home in Queens were getting looser and looser as he moved deeper into the gay subculture. His status in his adopted environment became an ever-larger part of his identity and self-esteem. His fantasies were no longer about the upper Amazon, but about cars and clothes and stereo sets and pudding-rich undemanding Johns. He walked a very empty street, and in the darkness of the night, he knew it.

But he didn't know what to do about it.

By the time Billy was seventeen, he had graduated from high school and gotten a job in the stock room of a distribution company in Manhattan. He lived sporadically with his parents, but he carried his toothbrush in his pocket and was likely to crash at anybody's pad, John or friend, at any hour of the night. The focus of his life was a couple of East Village soda joints and hamburger stands. Friday and Saturday night he cruised Fifty-third and Third. He had attained some kind of balance—precarious, but in a chaotic kind of way, livable. He had enough money to eat, a fall-back place to stay in his home in Queens, a workable system of emotional defenses, reasonable good health, and a steady flow of ego-inflation from his Johns. It was a life, of a sort. Dozens of kids he knew were living it, and their common knowledge tended to reinforce each other.

As he turned eighteen, Billy experienced the first of a series of shocks that put him through some deep changes.

For the first time in his life, he fell in love, and not with a girl either. A nubile fifteen-year-old chicken-queen with long blond hair, a turned-up nose, and flirtatious eyes. The queen was fem enough to give Billy the strange but reassuring feeling that he really was a girl, with certain minor variations of equipment, and that therefore he, Billy, was really straight. Billy felt strong, and butch, and protective, and fulfilled. He was dominant. Someone was dependent on him. And he controlled the situation —he thought—and the queen let him think so. At the soda joint and walking down Second Avenue or Bleecker Street, the queen snuggled close to him and let it be known to all his friends that She was His. It was a whole new ego trip and Billy enjoyed every minute of it . . .

Until, a week or so later, when the queen found some big butch number with a GTO and disappeared into the

kasbah of Brooklyn Heights. Billy saw her a couple of
nights later at a soda joint with the butch. They ran
through a scene or two from *Carmen;* the butch and Billy
got into a fight; Billy got 86ed from the joint, copped
some downs, skipped two days of work freaked out at
Jamie's fifth-floor walkup on East Third and Avenue B.

What happened at Jamie's those two days was the second big shock. Jamie was around twenty, tall, gaunt, and
gay. He had had a mild thing about Billy for some time,
but he hadn't pushed it. Since Billy hadn't started anything, Jamie had let it ride, knowing there might come a
time.

When Billy walked into Jamie's place, Jamie knew that
was the time. Billy's macho act had crumbled. He
lurched toward Jamie, put his arms around him, and just
held on. Jamie was different from the queen. Jamie was
different from the tricks. Jamie was different from Rodney. Jamie was a friend. Jamie was a man. And Billy
needed him.

Billy and Jamie had sex, but it was different from any
Billy had experienced. Jamie led, and Billy responded.
Then Billy led, and Jamie responded. In the interplay
there was no clear dominance or submission, but simply
a communication between equals, a fulfillment of needs
that each of them felt in common measure. It was a
healing thing.

But more. There was no way to avoid it or get around
it this time, no obfuscation of desire or motivation could
cloud the reality. He hadn't done it for the excitement,
or the money, or because Jamie was like a girl. He hadn't
just lain there in shielded dispassion. He had made love
to a guy because he wanted to. The guy had made love
to him, and he had wanted that, too. All the careful
illusions, self-deceptions, and rationalizations he had
cherished through the years lay cluttered at his feet and
he felt as naked in his spirit as he was in body.

"I gotta put on some clothes," he muttered to Jamie.
"Why?"
"Because . . . it's cold."
"It's over eighty."
"I feel cold."
"No you don't."
"I feel funny, running around without any clothes."
"Relax."
"Just my underpants?"
"No."
"I'm gonna."
"I'll rip them off."
"Yeah, you would, too."

Billy never did get his underpants on until he left Jamie's pad and walked out onto the street. He was careful walking down the street. He walked stiff-legged and butch, so nobody would know. But he knew.

Billy got himself a girl, a fine freaky head he picked up in Washington Square Park. He slept with her frequently and with enthusiasm for several weeks, trying to wipe out the remembrance of Jamie. He did pretty well at it until one night he and the girl went on an acid trip. It started out pleasantly enough, wandering through a Middle Earth poster, but in the middle of a field he had the sudden sensation of falling down through the earth into a vast vaulted cavern, dimly lit with street lamps, that he recognized as Central Park West. The floor of the cavern was covered with male bodies, still as they lay there, still as he had seen them on beds all over New York, young bodies and old, fat and thin, black and white, stretched and huddled, a great, slow-breathing carpet of flesh that extended out until it was lost in the shadows of the chamber. He moved slowly between the bodies, searching. He'd see faces; some of them he'd remember but others were strangers. At least he thought they were strangers. Maybe he'd slept with them once, but he couldn't remember. So many bodies. He could feel the heat of them in the chill of the cavern. He wanted to lie down and warm himself. But he had to keep hunting.

He was clambering, stumbling over the bodies. As he stepped on them, the bodies would cry out, grasp at him as he moved, and he'd struggle against them for holding him back. He had to keep moving. Until he found Jamie, lying there, entwined with a blond boy. He pulled back Jamie's head by the hair, but the eyes were blank, and when Billy let go, Jamie's head sank back and rested on the boy's shoulder. He cried out, but Jamie couldn't hear. He shook him, but Jamie didn't respond. Slowly, the boy's arm wrapped around Jamie's neck.

Billy moved on into the shadows and grottos, turning faces against the light and finding only strangers. He climbed over rocks, dank and cool with the drip of water, to find new chambers swirled in mists of acrid vapor. The moisture glinted on the skin and shapings of the arms and legs, torsos, and buttocks. Billy stumbled on through the mists till he saw a figure standing against the cavern wall, tall, lean, and familiar. It was Rodney. He called to him, but his voice was soundless. He stepped toward him, but hands held him back. He struggled against them, but more hands grasped him and pulled him down. In a swirl of thick mist, Rodney's figure disappeared.

Billy reared up again, moved on toward the farthest grotto. He didn't want to go, he knew that. He didn't want to find what he knew he would find. But he kept going. He picked his way down an incline as the ceiling of the cavern vaulted high above him, and he saw ahead of him a vast reach of solid rock, no way beyond. But the chamber, as he looked around, seemed empty. No bodies, there, no grappling hands, no sound.

Then he heard a voice, and knew whose it was. A voice as calm and reassuring as he had once heard it, a voice that could lead, and that he could follow, knowing that everything would be all right. It was the voice of his Uncle Mark, who had told him stories when he was a kid, long rambling stories in a deep resonant voice that conjured Indian spirits and the darks of forests. He would sit on his uncle's lap when he was a kid and hear the stories by the hour; he remembered the feel of him, the corded muscles on the back of his neck and the bush of his hair. He remembered his uncle's hand on his leg, and the gentle pressure.

Then . . . the time when it happened, and the other times. He had never told anybody.

He heard the voice, echoing against the rock, turned, and saw Mark, a body like his own, but tall and strong as he remembered. He ran to Mark, threw his arms around him, crying, felt Mark's arms around him and let the tears flow as he rested his head against Mark's chest.

"What's the matter?" the girl said. "Having a bad trip?"

And all Billy could say was "No. No. No. The greatest trip. The greatest."

"Why are you crying?"

"Because . . ."

After a while, he came down and went to sleep, his head on her chest. But he never slept with her again.

In Billy's case, the trip had been decisive. He knew who he was and where his head was at.

But Spunk, as usual, was ahead of him, had moved to the East Village and acquired a lover. He went to GAA meetings, wore a lambda button,[2] and once told Billy he was a closet queen. For which Billy nearly slugged him; it was a matter of pride. You don't call anybody a closet queen unless you smile first.

One evening Billy went over to see Spunk. Spunk's

[2]The Greek letter "lambda" is a symbol of Gay Liberation. A blue button, with an orange lambda inscribed, is frequently worn by militant gays.

lover was out, Spunk had gone through half a six-pack and was in a mood to dish somebody the tea. Billy was there, and it was Billy who got dished.

Billy made his initial mistake by mentioning the girl he'd been sleeping with, and what a cool girl she was. Spunk was ominously silent. Billy rambled on about the things she did, and how he liked it, and how she had a together head.

Spunk's question came flat-out. "You going straight?"

"Me?"

"Yeah, you."

Billy dodged. "Sometimes I like to sleep with girls."

"Big deal, but not what I asked you."

"So what's wrong with sleeping with girls?"

"Nothing . . . if you're straight. That's your bag."

"Who said I was straight?"

"I didn't say. I asked." A pause. "Well . . . ?"

"I'm gay. You know that."

"Then why all this heavy rap about a fish?"

"It's just . . . you know . . . something to talk about . . ."

"Shit."

"So why are you giving me a hard time?"

"Because you're still hanging in there in the fucking closet, is why."

"Not me."

"Yes, you. Sure, you'll hustle your ass off, just like I did, but when it comes to making it with somebody—really making it, and giving out—boy, how you back off!"

"I can make it."

"When?"

"Once."

"Then what happened?"

"I found the girl."

"Ha! Too much for you, huh?"

"She was cool."

"I don't mean the girl. I mean the guy—making it with the guy."

"I can make it again . . . with a guy."

"And give out, and be all there? Can you?"

"Yes!"

"Well, all right, if you're gay, get with it." Billy counterattacked. "So what's with you?"

"I make it."

"You like it?"

"No other way."

"For real?"

"Damn right."

"Tell me."

"What's there to tell?"

"You told me before . . . about Rodney."

"Long time ago."

"Now?"

"It's a whole different thing."

Billy kept thinking about that—"a whole different thing"— when he rang the buzzer to the apartment on Central Park West. A woman opened the door. He asked for Rodney, and she gave him an address in Brooklyn Heights. At the Brooklyn Heights address, a man answered the door. Rodney, it seemed, had just moved out. Billy was given an address on Gramercy Park. He took the subway back and went there. When the door opened this time, it was Rodney.

Billy said, "Hello, Rodney."

Rodney said, "Hello," and he hesitated just for a moment, "Billy."

Pause.

"Can I come in?"

"Sure. Come on in."

It was a big high-ceilinged apartment in an old brownstone. He recognized the furniture, though. Music was playing.

Rodney said, "You've grown up."

"It's been a while."

"Let me see. Almost three years."

"Gone through changes."

"We all do."

"I didn't know if I'd find you."

"You did."

"I wanted to."

"Oh?"

"I didn't know if you'd let me in . . . after the things I said."

"It's been a long time. How old are you now?"

"Nineteen. Be twenty in a couple of months."

"You came back. Why was that?"

"I don't know. Just wanted to find out how you were."

"I'm all right. How are you?"

"I'm all right, I guess."

There was an awkward pause as the two men stood in the middle of the living room, staring at each other. Billy averted his eyes for a moment, and then looked back at Rodney, hard. Rodney's stare softened. Billy knew. He stepped toward Rodney, and as they embraced, the signals went back and forth very fast. Billy, in effect, told Rodney that it was "a whole different thing," and Rodney, in effect, said he was ready for it. All it took was just one physical contact.

As there was a history of three years of changes behind Billy's statement, there was also a history behind Rodney's response. Only in the clear statement and clear response was the whole different thing going to be possible.

Rodney had been a late-bloomer. After an adolescence in which he had been highly ambivalent about his sexuality, he'd found a girl named Sandra in his senior year in college and after graduation married her. Sandra, he felt, would save him from his "darker self," and for several years Sandra, who was rapacious in her sexual appetites, did a pretty good job of it. She kept him on the verge of exhaustion most of the time.

But as Rodney moved up in his company, and took on new responsibilities, he had to travel. On lonely nights in Chicago, Washington, Boston, and Philadelphia, all his sexual ambivalence reemerged and his fantasies free-floated across boundaries that he had hoped and prayed were closed.

As the fantasies continued, he took long night walks through the streets and parks of cities, sat in bars, mostly straight, and waited, not wanting to go back to the hotel. Nothing happened for a long time, largely because when he felt a stare or a brush on his arm or a pressure on his leg or torso, he'd withdraw, and pull out of the circumstance as fast as possible. Solemnly he'd count the days, each trip, till he got back to Sandra.

The breakthrough came where he had least suspected it. Not on the streets or in the parks, but at the slide presentation of the fall product line of the company's national sales conference at the Ben Franklin Hotel in Philadelphia. As the lights lowered, Rodney found himself sitting next to a slim dark-haired man whom he had barely noticed. But in the darkness of the auditorium, the pressure on his leg was unmistakable. Rodney moved his leg. Pause. He felt a pressure on his arm. He let it rest. Pause. As the speaker reached a climax with the revelation of the national promotion budget that would make every last salesman's job an opportunity for a 50 percent monthly gross increase by Christmas, he felt the pressure on his leg again. He glanced to his side, saw the profile of the man next to him, a silhouette against the exit sign. Not bad. He shifted his body so that the pressure on the arm increased. In turn, the pressure on his leg increased. The rest of the process was a matter of arrangement, which led to the guy's room on the fifteenth floor, chaperoned by a bottle of bourbon.

The man's name was Randy and he was from the

branch office in Houston, Texas. *Texas?* A gay from Texas? Rodney found it difficult to believe that anyone from Texas could be gay, what with all that unlimited opportunity to sodomize long-horned cattle. How would a man have time for anything else? But here was this guy with this big badge on his lapel reading "Hello, my name is Randy and I'm from Houston, Texas." And how could you argue with that? Nor could Rodney argue with what happened afterward. It was a Wild West Show and he loved every minute of it.

The next day Randy and Rodney left Philadelphia at the conclusion of the sales meeting, and went back to their wives.

The episode with Randy had seemed, to Rodney, so natural and joyous—while it was happening. The retrospect was something else again. He was thrown off balance. His fantasies grew more garish, and more homosexual. While before he had counted the days until he could get back to Sandra after a field trip, he now counted the days he spent with Sandra in anticipation of the next field trip. His sexual communication with Sandra steadily diminished. His night excursions in other cities grew more searching, more intense, and at times, more desperate. What he found was a weird miscellany of experience, bereft of sense, meaning, or fulfillment. But he still kept hunting. There *was* somebody out there like Randy, he told himself; he just couldn't find him.

He broke up with Sandra within the year. There were no children, and the ties between them had grown very thin. Their parting was a muted, pathetic thing; Sandra had long since found somebody else; Rodney had found Central Park West.

Shortly thereafter, after he had been ripped off by one hustler and beaten by another, he found Billy, aged sixteen, lately of Queens, and in a state of relative innocence. It was a star-crossing. Two lives had entangled at a particular stage in the development of each. The intensity of the need that each of them felt gave the relationship, even though it lasted only a month or so, a very special significance in each of their lives. As Rodney had thereafter cropped up in Billy's thoughts, dreams, and the acid trip, so Billy had found a niche in Rodney's fantasies that kept recurring in the years that followed their separation. Each of them became the other's myth.

At the same time, though they never saw each other, their developmental patterns paralleled. They both went through their promiscuities; Billy as a chicken, Rodney as a chicken-hawk. They both went through their macho self-delusions of straightness. (For a time, for instance, Rodney had dated a girl, but before the moment of truth had come, he was much relieved to find out that she was as gay as he was and the relationship flourished as a mutual convenience.) They both had been read out by their fellow gays.

When Rodney and Billy embraced, the stars, nearby all along, crossed again in a different part of the sky. Their needs were quite different now, but just as intense, and the mythology with which each had surrounded the other gave the reunion a homecoming sense of rightness. They were both ready for an honest no-nonsense homosexual relationship.

What would happen? Who knows? One could run through a dozen scenarios. The issue here is how they came to the point of departure—the whole different thing. Here again, there are a dozen, a hundred, a thousand different scenarios, and the story of Billy is just one of them.

But imbedded in Billy's story, and myriad ones like it, is a dynamite issue. Call it proselytizing or what you will, the issue is how and when and under what circumstances the older, more experienced gay, or the gay community in general, impinges on the free-floating individual. I've watched this one carefully. As far as I have been able to see, the individual has to make a considerable effort to get into the scene. The individual has to make the first move, the second move, the third move, and more before people are going to take much notice of him. Like any in-group, gays seem to have their initiation period, and the activities of the individual are limited to one- or two-night stands that he either elicits or consents to. Sure, older gays may make a considerable courtship display to get some young chicken into bed, but the process is as likely to be the other way around, and the earliest reminiscence of most gays I know includes the phrase— "and then *I* seduced *him*."

But just what the hell is this "seduction" thing anyway? I've never been "seduced" if I didn't want to be "seduced," nor ever "seduced" anyone who wasn't sending out a rash of signals that whatever happened was going to be just jim-dandy by him. There may be a lot of horseplay along the line, but the basic mutual consent seems to be established very early in the process. If there isn't mutual consent, that, too, can be established before things get out of hand. Courtship display is simply a statement of willingness and interest on one side of the counter. What happens on the other side of the counter determines whether an agreement is going to be reached.

Yet at some point along the line the individual's kindred spirits in the gay community are likely to come down on him like a ton of brick. At least as I've observed it, the one thing committed gays can't stand is one of the brothers flimflamming around . . . for too long. A certain amount of "I'm straight, man, straight" will be tolerated as the individual plays around gay bars, soda joints, Fifty-third and Third, and Christopher Street, but the time comes when, in the opinion of his confreres, enough is enough. "If you're straight, man, be straight, but don't hang around these parts. If you're gay—and we know you're gay—then it's time to say it loud and clear." The reading-out can be gentle and kidding or tough and traumatic, but whatever the form, the message is the same—"Either establish your identity and make the scene, or get out of the scene." Some bridle for a time. Most make it. The final step toward gay identity has been taken, and with that consciousness the capacity to move into the whole different thing that is the substance of homosexual life. The point is that the impingement of the gay community on the free-floating individual is most likely to take place at the final border line. It is not a procreative process; it is an obstetrical process. The phrase "coming out" reflects the reality.

Chapter Eight

The process of coming out that is likely to take place in late adolesence is, for a gay going into his twenties and into the substantive gay subculture, a part of his history. Like all history, it exerts deep and not easily definable influences on present attitudes, present behavior, and present perceptions of reality. What was is part of what's now, and it is sometimes tough to cope with.

When tall black Vernon was in residence, he brought around one evening one of the most exotically beautiful human beings I had ever seen. Carlos walked in as if he were entering a sacred chamber of an Aztec temple, and I could see the glint of silver, hear the tinkle of ceremonial bells and the rustle of a feathered cloak. He sat down on the couch as if it were a throne. I sat there, like a fool, and gawked. Land 'o Goshen, where did Vernon *get* things like this?

In point of fact, he didn't have on a feathered cloak but in contrast to the denim bells, work shirts, suede jackets and heavy belts and boots endemic to the scene, he might as well have. He wore full pleated slacks right out of the twenties, a body shirt and neck scarf. His hair was long, black, and lustrous. His face was right off the wall of a pre-Columbian temple, long lost in the jungles of the Yucatan.

As it turned out, I'd missed it by a thousand miles or so. Carlos was Peruvian, and I was not to play Cortes, but Pizarro, debauching the treasures of the Incas. But that comes later, and, as a matter of fact, I'm still wondering just who debauched who. Like Pizarro in *Royal Hunt of the Sun*, I have a suspicion. . .

Vernon and I sat there, sharing the gossip on the Rialto, while Carlos sized up the apartment, detail by detail. At last he noted that it was a very beautiful apartment and went on to suggest, in tones befitting Inca royalty, that I should move out so that he could move in. I in turn suggested that Scots, being privy to the Almighty through prayer and Calvin, are not easily pushed, but . . . and the pause just hung there for a moment . . . "I have an alternative suggestion."

Vernon went six inches out of his chair and came down slapping his thigh. "I knew it. I knew it. I knew it!" As usual, Vernon did.

About six weeks after Carlos' first appearance, he reappeared, and ensconced himself in the living room. I had another visitor that evening, and the conversation went its way. But in the course of it, Carlos made some discreet inquiries about the whereabouts of Vernon. I told him that Vernon had recently departed to the wilds of the East Village, and there the matter rested.

Two days later, Carlos showed up again. This time the occasion involved the nitty-gritty. Since he couldn't move me out, and didn't have the money for the rent anyway, he had decided to take me up on the alternative suggestion and move himself in. Huh. Okay. So was a peasant like me going to object to a visit from Inca royalty? Anyway, that was the first impression. Other impressions quickly followed.

For one thing, Carlos had a problem. The first night, he revealed the problem. It was clear to me that his penis was about to fall off, which was a depressing thought. He said he was allergic to downs. I said he should get the hell up to the VD clinic as fast as possible. Our nuptial night we spent at some distance on either side of the waterbed, and the next morning he repaired to the clinic at Twenty-eighth Street and Ninth Avenue. It must have been some scene when Carlos showed up! I had been there once, and while it was remarkably businesslike, it was also pretty Russian. You sit in the waiting room with ten or fifteen other men, and a lot of cruising goes on. (Cruising? In a *VD clinic*? Habit carried to excess!) This stalwart fellow comes in and in a loud voice says, "Okay, all of you guys that are dripping, follow me!" The sheep follow him, as a Judas goat, to the needle.

Several hours later, Carlos returned with a very humpy number who turned out to be a social worker from the clinic. Carlos might, or might not, have been allergic to downs, but what he had was syphilis. It had been going on for months. The social worker had come on the delicate mission of finding out just who Carlos had shared his pleasures with for the past five months. That social worker, his eyes glistening, just couldn't wait to find out!

The conference that followed was an unusual exercise in mnemonics; the social worker sitting, pencil poised on a foolscap pad, and Carlos, regally vague. Well . . . there was this guy named George . . . I think his name was George . . . and he had this place on Seventeenth Street with a sleeping loft that held six. . . . His last name? . . . Something Irish, I think . . . Mc somethingorother.

. . . Yes, I think I'd recognize the house. And so forth and so on.

With about a half a dozen names in hand, Carlos and the social worker set out on their Public Health Mission through the warrens and walkups of downtown New York. While Carlos waited in the car, the social worker would go on his errands of mercy. "I'm here from the Public Health Department, and we just want to let you know that you have been exposed to syphilis and we recommend you come down to the clinic for treatment." And a Merry Christmas to one and all!

Carlos was a painter, and a good one. He'd hunch over a corner of the living room with a sketch pad, a set of water colors, and a box of Q-Tips, and turn the stuff out like a printing press. He was heavy into the gay thing, and most of what came out was plain and fancy, long and short, thick and thin, redwhiteandblue penises. Carlos was evidently out to rectify the long artistic neglect of this particular part of the human anatomy, and he really worked at it. Every time he'd finish a sketch, he'd post it somewhere on the living-room walls or in the bedroom area and the place began to look like an Istanbul peghouse.

But after a while, Carlos felt confined by two dimensions and decided to go on to phallic 3-D, which involved carpentry, chicken-wire, and plaster of paris—all in the living room. Which led me to some dark speculations about the comparative disadvantages of living with a dancer or a graphic artist. What did I want, a gym or a junk yard? High culture, underfoot, had its price.

But nothing that happened in the living room prepared me for Carlos' pad in the East Village. After a week or so of residence at my place, Carlos decided that the new ground was sufficiently secure to break up his other place. We took a car I had at the time and went over to East Third Street, climbed some dank stairs, and entered a chaos of squalor to chill the soul. Carlos, that impeccable Inca regality, had been living in a llama pen.

Carlos' roommate had been a drag-queen named Bunny who had decamped for Florida, leaving her detritus behind her, packets of powder, little bottles of this and that, a wig or two, bra and underpants, nail polish, and a miscellany of china animals. Carlos, in turn, contributed a miscellany of sulpture, half-finished bottles of paint, canvases, brushes, and whatnot. The dishes were stacked in the sink in layers of geological time. The place had last been cleaned in the Pleistocene Epoch. Carlos wandered around distractedly, like a lost boy, picking up one thing, putting it down, and picking up something else. Suddenly he discovered on the floor a ripped drawing of an amply endowed older woman. He picked up the pieces. "Bunny could have done anything to me . . . but *not* my Sophie Tucker drawing!"

I remembered the first time he had been at the house he'd talked about his place with a great deal of pride, how he was fixing it up, painting it, the furnishings he was going to get for it, and indeed there were a few pieces—a chair, a table—that looked as if they had once had some attention, but they were buried under accumulations of junk.

What had happened? Carlos shrugged. "It was all right for a while, and then I got lonely. Bunny needed a place, and I took him in. He had this drag thing. And I like to look good. So I guess all we got to care about was how we looked when we went out the door." He looked around. "I didn't think it would get like this."

Out the door. Two sides of the door. Private self and public self. What the Johns, lovers, admirers, and passers-by thought about Carlos, and what he thought about himself. On the outside of the door he had plenty to respond to, and he could put on a front that could dazzle the Sphinx. But inside the door, alone or with Bunny, the whole thing had just come apart at the seams. I began to understand more clearly than ever before how all the flattery and ego-inflation lavished on a public self can overload the circuits of a personality to the point of serious dysfunction.

For the next six months that Carlos was in residence I watched him, in fits and starts, put himself together. The changes he went through looked like a fifty-year graph of the stock market. But throughout all the turmoil, he kept sketching and painting and went through a hyperthyroid history of modern art—from Rouault, through Whistler, on to Chagall, around to Munch, with a quick stop at Matisse, a bow to Burne-Jones, and a big huzzah for Aubrey Beardsley—with very little formal art training, but an awful lot of raw talent.[1]

Life with Carlos included about the only close contact I ever had with the drag phenomenon. After Carlos went through his penis period, he got into a lot of portraits of women. The faces were all hauntingly similar—sad, faded, world-weary, angular, and heavily made up, right out of a third-rate bar in Berlin in the twenties. That face was Carlos' alter-ego. He called her Monique.

"When I'm her, I'm different. I'm out of myself. I'm another person, and I can do things I can't do when I'm me. It's just I can take a vacation from myself. She's there, waiting for me, every time I want to be her. When I put on the dress, makeup, and wig, it's as if it was all there, all along, and I just fit myself into her and nobody can find me because I'm her. She's beautiful. She's been around. She knows. And I feel that way when I'm her."

I never saw Carlos in drag; I never wanted to. Carlos as male was quite sufficient unto the day. If I'd wanted a woman, I'd have gotten myself a woman. But Carlos' thing about Monique was real and for a while—merci-

[1]As of this writing, would you believe a canvas on exhibit at the Whitney? I certainly didn't, until I saw it there in a student exhibit.

fully, a short while—he was into it heavily. Dresses in the closet and wigs in the bottom drawer of the chest. (There's something damn spooky about finding a wig in a bottom drawer; there might be a head underneath it.) The Monique phase reached a climax when Carlos, egged on by some friends of his, decided to settle the issue once and for all at the Monday Night Drag Show at the Gold-Bug, one of the then better-known gay bars in the Village. He was going to show them that Monique could hold her own with the best. He got himself rigged out in a red and black number, went over there, gave one performance, blew their minds, and the next day went out and bought himself a pair of straight-legged jeans. That, said Carlos, was that, and as far as I know, he's never been in drag since.

But what was this identity bit he went through with Monique? Was it just pure escape from ennui? Or the final sloughing-off of the queen image he had been into in late adolescence? Or a big urge to bask in some adulation at a rather low point in his life, adulation that he didn't feel he could elicit in his identity as Carlos? Why Monique came is one question. Maybe it had something to do with androgens, and the lack thereof. But why Monique went is another question, and I have this hunch that the assertive energy which Carlos was putting into his art had a lot to do with Monique's demise. For whatever reason, he just didn't need her anymore.

The conflict between Carlos' public and private selves continued, a constant alternation between arrogant self-confidence and agonizing self-doubt that is characteristic of a lot of creative people. But with Carlos, the ups and downs were accentuated by the facts of gay life. Not that Carlos' gayness as such constituted any particular problem. He had come out years before, knew where his head was at, and was quietly militant about it. The problem was that an awful lot of people wanted to get into his pants and were willing to use any blandishment available to succeed. Despite Carlos' "I'm the greatest" protestations, which sometimes sounded for all the world like Mohammed Ali warming up for a prizefight, Carlos really wasn't all that sure of himself and his talent, and needed encouragement. He grabbed it wherever he could get it and would build himself up and up and up, and then, having sense enough to realize that most of what he was getting was unreal, would come crashing down again. It was tough to live with; it was, I'm sure, a lot tougher to live through. A lot of times I'd wake up in the middle of the night to find Carlos lying there, wide awake, staring at the ceiling. As Fitzgerald wrote, "In the real dark night of the soul it is always three o'clock in the morning."

Carlos, relatively early in his stay with me, got himself a studio and decided to have a show. He had a pretty good stock of paintings already, but there weren't enough male nudes to suit him, and he did six weeks' intensive work to get ready for the exhibit. The whole idea was to make some money to keep the studio going and have a steady flow of supplies.

As the date for the show came closer, tension mounted. His output of sketches, watercolors, and acrylics was impressive. He'd invite his friends over to inspect his work, and they'd give him flattering encouragement. On he'd go, working eight, nine, ten hours a day. We had invitations made up and sent out, a price list put together, and Cory, who was around at that time, helped Carlos get the studio cleaned up and in shape. It was quite a project. By opening night his adrenaline was up near the top of the register. He was going to *make it,* by God, and nothing was going to stop him now. Opening night all his friends and relations came, looked around, and said all the right things. Carlos glowed. But as the evening wore on, the terrible truth became more and more evident. With the exception of two people who bought $10 watercolors, nobody was buying.

The show was going on two more evenings, and Carlos kept telling himself and me that the buyers would be coming the second and third nights. But on the second and third nights Carlos spent most of his time alone at the studio, waiting for people who never came. (Too bad; I have a suspicion that some smart people could have picked up some pretty good investments.)

The effect on Carlos was devastating. The down lasted for weeks. He fell back in with an old tribe of friends whose futility was equaled only by their inertia. They'd all sit around the studio or someone's house and indulge in a curious form of vocalization that can only be called "queen patter." The object of the vocal exercise is to say as little as possible in as long a time as possible. One queen establishes the basic theme, like: What happened to my third pair of pants? Or: What drag-queen is modeling for *Vogue* this month? Or: Who was that tired troll I saw you with at Danny's last night? Once the basic theme has been established, the variations are endless and can go on for hours, all in a lilting murmur of sound signifying nothing.

A couple of weeks of queen patter, and Carlos had had a bellyful. He went back to his art work and got into a whole new period. Through some strange set of circumstances, he managed to land a commission to do a mural on someone's apartment walls. The clients were apparently as intrigued with Carlos as they were with the prospect of a mural. But it was a commission and Carlos needed it. He revved up again, as he had before the first art show, but this time the disenchantment with flattery began to show as well as a healthy caution about his talent.

"That damn wall is ten feet by twenty feet. That's a big wall! What the hell am I going to put on it?"

I could just see those poor clients trying to live with Carlos' version of an Orozco, and urged pastels.

Carlos littered the desk with sketches, some of which were lousy and he knew it. "It's not that I can't do it. I know I can do it. I just don't *believe* I can do it, you know what I mean?"

I allowed as how I did.

"All the shit going on all around," he went on. "I hear it. I know it. People keep telling me, you know, how good I am. Yeah, but what does it mean? I've got to *believe* it myself that I can do it. I keep trying. But it's rough. I mean, I don't know. I do, but I don't, right down where it counts."

But somehow he did it—all twenty feet of wall. Other commissions followed, along with the hanging at the Whitney, and Carlos was on his way.

Carlos' exorcism of the demons attendant on the coming-out process was relatively mild. His work held him together, and, regardless of the ups and downs, kept him moving. He could put the blandishments of gay life in some kind of perspective, and the pressure of his work kept his feet somewhere near the ground. The history of his coming out was just that—history— and relegated to his life's background.

But with other gays, history was front and center, a constant presence that festered and distorted present action. Exorcism came hard for Martin.

My acquaintaince with Martin started with needing a belt to go with the jeans I had just bought. I dropped into a Village leather store to pick one out. The place was empty except for a long-haired head behind the counter, absorbed in some leather-making equipment. Not wanting to interrupt creativity, I went over to the belt rack to figure out what I wanted.

"Can I help you?" The voice had a gentle southern lilt.

I looked around. He had big china-blue eyes and a kind of hound-dog way of watching—observant, patient, sad, but finally unfathomable. His face was smooth-shaven but with pockmarks that gave him a slightly damaged quality, enhanced by a ragged denim shirt and a heavy leather arm band that was studded and battered. He was probably in his early twenties but he seemed ageless.

We stared at each other a long moment.

"I need a new belt."

He stepped out from behind the counter. He was slight of build, almost fragile, and he wasn't very tall. But I got a sense of resigned durability; he was down but not out.

"We've got quite a few here," he said. "If you don't find one you like, maybe I could make one up for you."

I tried on several, as he handed them to me. He stood close. His voice was low. Our eyes met occasionally, and it was usually mine that turned away. There was something very strange about his stare, as if he was trying to find something in the back of my retina. What I felt was just as strange, like I wanted to be with him alone on the top of a mountain.

He held out another belt, and I noticed a bruise on his arm, a crescent of discolored flesh at the cuff of his short-sleeved shirt. As his arm moved, the whole bruise showed. Teeth marks were visible. He pulled his arm back so that the shirt covered the bruise again, and his eyes turned away.

I found a belt I liked.

We stood there, awkwardly. He took his time coiling the belt and putting it in a bag. I couldn't think of anything to say, until . . . "I'll need a receipt," I said as I handed him the money.

He nodded, brought out a pad, put the carbon in carefully. He wrote the amount. I gave him my name and address. He wrote that carefully, handed me the original, and kept the carbon.

"I live right around here," I said. "Drop by if you want."

He gave me that hound-dog look, and then the trace of a smile as I left the store.

By nine that evening he had appeared at the front door. No one was in residence at the time. The place was tomb-quiet. He moved around the room like a ghost, and then settled himself on the couch. I asked him if he'd like a drink and he said he would, and that was the start of a very long weekend.

No big thing about the gay bit. That was established before the first drink was finished when he swung around on the couch and stretched out full length with his head on my lap. I put my hand on his chest and he winced. I took my hand away. He pulled it back. "Not there. Here." And put it on another part of his chest, keeping his hand on top of mine.

"You been in some kind of accident?" I asked.

"Call it that."

"What happened?"

"I'm out of it now."

"Heavy?"

"Yeah. But it's over."

I let it drop. The room was full of peculiar vibes that I kept telling myself I didn't understand. I kept having these big flooding urges, rushes almost, to guard him, to protect him, to stave off whatever evil spirits lurked to hurt him.

I looked down at him. He was gazing up at me. His eyes were big and damp. Outside the traffic rumbled, but the quiet inside the house was palpable, and in the beats of time, neither of us moved. Then suddenly he reared up, gulped the rest of his drink, and disappeared into the john. He came back a few moments later, his face flushed from rinsing, sat in a chair bolt upright, and asked for another drink. When I handed it to him, he looked a long time at the glinting liquid in the glass.

"My name is Martin."

"Hi."

"I don't know why I came here."

"Because I suggested it."

"That just says what you did. Not what I did."

"All right, why did you come?"

"I don't know. I don't think I should have. I think I've got to go."

"Finish your drink first."

"I don't want to get boozed up again."

"Again?"

"Last night. Night before that. It's been going on all week."

"Sometimes that's the way to get rid of . . . what you've got to get rid of."

"I'm never going to get rid of it."

He took a long gulp of his drink, then looked at me with that hound-dog look again. "Who are you?"

"Wallace."

"Where are you from?"

"Here."

"You don't sound like you're from New York."

"I've traveled around some."

"Ever been in Virginia?"

"Passing through."

"I'm from Virginia."

"Beautiful state."

"Parts of it, I guess."

"When did you leave?

"Nearly five years now. I never want to go back."

I let it drop again. He had this strange way of shutting doors. But every time one would shut, another would open, and there he'd be, peeking out at me with those big eyes.

He got up, went over to the kitchen counter, poured himself another drink. He turned and what he said he seemed to be saying to himself. "Monday night I left. I came back Tuesday. I left again Wednesday. Here it is Friday." He looked around the room as if he were waking up in a strange place. "He went crazy. He wouldn't stop. That's why I left. Got myself this room. Lousy hotel. Look at the walls. Keep thinking about him. How it felt. I got to get out of that bag."

I got up to pour myself a drink.

He said, "The belt looks good on you." He reached over and slowly unbuckled it.

"What are you doing?"

He didn't answer. He just pulled the belt off, held it in his hand. Then he doubled it over and offered it to me. "You want to beat me?"

"No."

"It's kicks."

"Not for me."

"He did it."

"And you left."

"He wouldn't stop." He hesitated. "You'd stop, when I told you, wouldn't you?"

"I'm not starting. It's not my thing."

"You looked like it was, there in the store."

"Is that why you came?"

"Yes." A long pause. "No. Another reason."

"What's that?"

"You're not kidding? You're not a master?"

"No."

"You don't want to beat me?"

"Hell, no."

"You just like to make love . . . without . . . ?"

"Hurting people turns me off."

He looked puzzled. "Been a long time since I met anybody like you."

"We do exist."

"I keep hunting. But all I get is guys who like to beat me."

"Because you hunt for them."

"I guess so."

"And you like it."

He held the belt in his hands, stretched it between his two fists until his knuckles were white. Then, in a sudden explosion of energy, threw it across the room. "*No!*" He lurched across the room, braced himself in a corner. "No. No. No. No. I didn't do anything! What did I do? First it was his belt, and he was using the buckle. Then the whip. He's got me tied down and I'm begging him, telling him, screaming at him . . . *to stop!* It's hurting like it's white hot and going through me and the sound's all in my ears like a siren and I can't hear and I can't see . . . all I can do is feel . . . the hurt . . . like a charge . . . that's going to kill me! Why's he want to kill me? What did I do? It wasn't to him. He didn't know. Nobody knows except me. And I've had it enough! The hurt and all! For what I did!"

"What did you do?"

He looked at me as if he were seeing me for the first time and that what he was seeing was a ghost. He covered his face with his hands and started moaning. His whole body shook. Then he dropped his hands. His eyes focused on mine, he crossed the room with slow uncertain steps, and collapsed into my arms.

I wasn't exactly sober myself, but I got him into bed. His body looked like a battlefield of welts, bruises, and scars that crisscrossed his chest, stomach, and thighs. Looking at him there beside me, his eyes closed, breathing heavily, looking at the wreckage of a beautiful body, I felt a black helpless rage. I held him. I kissed him. I covered him against whatever it was that could harm him.

His eyes opened. His hand ran through my hair. "It's all right." His voice was almost serene. "I'm here, with you. And you're with me."

We made love. It was one of those beautiful things that sometimes happen.

I woke up early the next morning to find Martin bunched up into a defensive ball on the far side of the bed. I lay there for a few moments, contemplating the complexities of buying a belt. Suddenly, he sat bolt upright in bed and stared at me.

"What's the problem?" I asked.

"I got to get going."

"It's only six-thirty in the morning."

"I got to go."

He got up and dressed. His eyes were downcast and they never met mine. I got such weird vibrations of guilt that I even checked my wallet, but all my money was there. Something was drastically wrong, and I hadn't the foggiest idea what. "You want to talk about something?"

"What?"

"Whatever's bugging you."

"No."

"Would you like to come back tonight?"

"No.

He mumbled thanks as he went out the door. I was left feeling desolate.

At nine that evening, I heard a knock on the door and there stood Martin. He was stoned on something. From the smell of him, it was a combination of beer and grass. He kissed me like he meant it, said he was sorry about what had happened, announced that he was fucked up in the head, and headed for the liquor bottle. I could see it was going to be another nice quiet evening at home with Martin, another quick run-through of the decline and fall of the Roman Empire. Ridiculous, but I was delighted to see him.

We got drunk and went to bed. But it was the same story as that morning, with Martin making a defense of the Alamo over in a corner of the bed. I was in no mood for siege tactics and let it be known that if he didn't like it around here, he could take himself elsewhere. With that edict, I rolled over and set up my own Alamo on the other side of the bed.

Silence.

Then a stirring.

Then I felt Martin's body next to mine. Here we go again. "Damnit, I want to know what's going on. Now, tell me."

"You're you. I have to keep telling myself that."

"Right on. I'm me. So who do you think I am?"

"You're big, like he was."

"Who?"

"You feel like he felt."

"Who?" The suspicion was beginning to crawl up my spine.

"A man I knew."

"And slept with?"

"Yes."

"Who?"

"No."

"Get it out."

"No!"

"So you go on getting yourself beaten. Why?"

" 'Cause I need to be punished."

"Why?"

"Because I slept with him."

"Who?"

His breathing was fast and shallow.

"For Chrissakes, get it out of your system! Who?"

The words came in choking spasms. "My father. And

he died. I did it. Because of that. Have to be punished. Because I did it. He's dead. And I loved him."

The sobs came in great wrenches, and they went on and on, shaking and twisting his body. Martin's anguish gradually spent itself and he was quiet. After a while I asked if he wanted to talk about it.

A long pause. "Yes."

We lay there in the darkness and he talked. "I know. It wasn't me. It wasn't what we did. The truck . . . it lost its brakes. Dad was ahead of the truck in his own car. The truck just went over him. It took a blowtorch to get him out. The truck. It was like lightning, or a roll of the dice, or God or something. God? Why did He do that? Nothing left. A body, all crushed up. His body." His voice stopped.

"I've lost some people, too," I said.

"Dead?"

"Gone."

"Did He do that? I mean, God?"

"No help from Him. Did it all by myself."

"I didn't do it. I know that now. *I didn't do it!* But I did, you see? After what happened, that *had* to happen! Truck. Could have been anything. I did it. I did it. *I did it!*"

I reared out of bed, went over to the corner of the room, picked up the belt, brought it back to the bed, and handed it to him. "Go ahead, beat me!"

He stared at the belt, then at me, his face shadowed in the night light.

I said, "Go ahead, chickenshit. I did it, too! Go ahead, beat me!"

He took the belt, folded it carefully, and handed it back. "You bought it to hold up your pants. It's a good belt. It'll hold up your pants. Put it someplace. You'll need it in the morning."

I put it on top of the bureau.

"Now, come here," he said, and held out his arms.

The next morning, he said thanks, and then he said good-bye. "I think I can go back to Virginia now." He closed the door and that was the last I ever saw of him.

Chapter Nine

Before I moved to New York and was still ensconced in the closet down in Maryland, I had business dealings with three young men from New York. Craig was one of them, the other two were Max and Kerry. Sitting across conference tables from them, I sized them up. Craig and Kerry were straight. Max was gay. The assessment, it turned out, was less than brilliant. Craig and Kerry were gay. Max was straight. What the hell, you can't win 'em all.

When I came to New York and got in touch with them, I was still cherishing my delusions. But then again, they had their delusions, too. They had me all sized up as Mr. Straight-Arrow himself.

Somehow I managed to keep the trio apart from the Corys and the Bruces and the others who decorated the establishment. But then one evening, Kerry came over with a bottle of Scotch, and the fun started. I was in a loquacious mood and the talk rambled on about life in the Village. At one point I made a passing reference to Danny's. As I kept on talking, I caught Kerry looking at me, clinically. At a pause, he said, "You mentioned Danny's. Is that the one on Christopher Street?"

"Sure, right down by the PATH entrance."

He looked stunned. "Wallace, are you gay?"

"Of course. Are you?"

"Of course."

"Well, how 'bout that?" At which point, Kerry started my education on another if somewhat less exotic aspect of the gay subculture than I was used to—the Upper East Side type gays in their early twenties who were Kerry's specialty.

Kerry, like Craig, had a genius for pickups—anywhere, anyhow, any time. While Craig came on like the handsome aristocrat, Kerry came on like everybody's swinging Dutch uncle. Just as the blacks that Craig liked found him quite irresistible as the embodiment of the American Dream, so the Upper East Side types warmed themselves in Kerry's bouyant confidence. Kerry emanated emotional authority. For willowy gays who had little themselves, Kerry's strength and assurance must have had a very special attraction. I saw that attraction at work as we made the rounds of the Village gay bars that evening. I could stomp into one of those places and the vibrations of nonattention would be thunderous. But making the rounds with Kerry was to bask in reflected glory. We'd walk in, a hush would fall, heads would turn, and Kerry would take over. The first step would be to establish a bridgehead with the bartender. After the bartender was mobilized, Kerry would then give his attention to the talent on the customer's side of the bar. Exchanges of matches, cigarettes, drinks, weather reports, and mutual admiration would ensue, with at least four or five people getting into the act. I'd stand there beside him, with a warm and friendly glower on my face, and watch the goings-on with awe.

The people who gravitated to Kerry were very different from the exotics I cherished. They tended to be in their early or mid-twenties, slim, well dressed in body shirts and skin-tight denims, with a well-bred grace and quietude about them. I had this feeling that I was watching a movie of antelope or gazelles grazing on the veldt. These were deer people. Beautiful they were; exciting they were not. But Kerry reveled in them, and could attract them like bees to clover.

As the evening wore on, and the communion of our common experience grew, it came time for *terrible confessions,* self-revelations that would strain and challenge the strength of our friendship. Standing at the fifth gay bar of our evening's rounds, I looked him keenly in the eye. What would he say when I told him? Would he bridle and change the subject? Would he cut me dead and walk out? I had to know. If we were to go on with our relationship, he would have to confront the darkest of my desires, and either accept it for what it was, or send me on my way with charity. I had to know.

"You know something, Kerry?"

"What?"

"I didn't want to tell you this before, but what the hell, now that I'm in New York, you'd better know. I like to play bridge."

"You do?"

"And I haven't played bridge in a long, long time."

"You haven't?"

"Kerry, do you like to play bridge?"

"I certainly do."

"Well, do you suppose that among all these beautiful people that we've seen this evening there might be two other people who like to play bridge?"

"I should certainly think so," he said.

And that's how we started Murder, Inc. The lethal events are, in fact, still going on at present writing and Sunday afternoons are still the despair of those not involved. Said somebody's lover, "I can't figure out how four adult males can sit around for five hours, slaughtering each other, and then kiss each other good-bye." Well, that's bridge. I mean, what the hell, when your partner gets you up to six clubs and all he's got is three to the jack and an outside ace? Call it justifiable homicide.

At any rate, the composition of the bridge group kept changing periodically, and that's how I got to know the deer-people. They led considerably more stable lives than the gypsies I knew. Each of them had a lover with whom he might have lived for six months or a year, and he'd bring him along. Hence what was going to be a quartet would end up as a fair-sized roomful of people, with those not involved moving in and out during the course of the afternoon. It was all very domestic, but quite incomprehensible to straight friends who occasionally dropped by. What were all those floaters doing, just hanging around? Well, Harry's with Charlie, and George is with Ben, and Randall is living with Kenneth, and they don't want to be separated on weekends, right? Well . . . now that I think about it . . .

Meanwhile, back at the bridge table, the blood-letting would continue, but as partners would be changed after each rubber, the nonplayers would shift around too, so that Harry was still next to Charlie, George next to Ben, and Randall next to Kenneth. I was fascinated with the precision of the fidelities, and the well-bred gentility of it all. Members of my tribe would either be trying to sit in one's lap, or off roistering around in Washington Square Park. Not these fellows. They just sat there in marital patience, exchanging extrasensory sweet-nothings with their chosen ones.

The other thing that impressed me was that they all tended to look alike and act alike. There were none of those big-pendulum swings of age, background, and personality that I was familiar with. The difference between lovers seemed, on the surface at least, to be minuscule, and maybe that was one factor in the relative stability of the bonding. Roles could be changed with comparative ease and in an interplay between equals, tradeoffs could be balanced. Among these deer-people who was playing doe at any particular moment and who was playing buck didn't seem to matter all that much.

These modes of mature homosexuality were well beyond the turmoils of coming out and prior to the anguishes of conscious aging. This, for these deer-people, was high noon, the meridian of what they had struggled to achieve.

Why was it so damn dull? Was I so hyped up with the freaks of my tribe that I couldn't appreciate a happy stasis when I saw it? I remembered knowing happy straight couples long ago and they, too, were pretty dull. Is tranquil happiness always so sodden when viewed from the outside? I've come to the conclusion that 90 percent is the fault of my own vision, a natural proclivity for change, despair, and ecstasy that almost precludes imagining (except for life with Vernon and a few others) the possibility of contentment. But seeing it there, around the bridge table, I've been bothered about that 10 percent that may not be the fault of my vision.

Just how durable is a placid relationship? Just how alive is a happiness cherished and cloistered and held glowing in some bell jar, protected against turmoil? I had the strange feeling that these deer-people had worked so hard to find what they had that they were in danger of suffocating it in order to preserve it. Here, if it was so, was a real pathos, a not-so-visible way-station along the road toward liberation.

Kerry was an exception to the post-coming-out marital

domesticity around the bridge table. Kerry liked his freedom and used it to remarkable effect. Sure, he had his
repeaters, but for the most part, it was a new one every
night. Occasional visitations of the clap slowed him
down, but he'd be back in business in a week going as
strong as ever. Every so often he'd mention one of his
conquests three or four times over a period of time, and
I'd begin to suspect that he was getting into something.
But the fancy would pass. "What ever happened to Joe?"
I'd ask.

"Joe who?"

"The one you went to Fire Island with."

"Oh, *that* Joe. Yeah, well, I guess he's around."

That would be that as far as Joe was concerned, because this week it was Jonathan, and next week, who
knows?

Kerry's alley-cat ways seemed to fit the stereotype of
the promiscuous, ever-searching, bed-to-bed gay who
was driven by loneliness and an incapacity for durable
relationship. His actions fitted the pattern, but *he* didn't.
Kerry gave every indication of thoroughly enjoying himself, and each new conquest was a discovery to be explored and savored. But Kerry had an oriental concern
about "face" that showed up in all sorts of ways. Was this
savor of conquest just a great big front behind which a
very lonely guy was hiding? Were all the recitals of conquest songs to his own ego embroidered with fantasies
of what-could-have-been? Possibly, but the weight of the
evidence was against this interpretation. As Carlos said
admiringly, "Kerry is a fine happy roll in the hay," and
I had no reason to disbelieve him.

But, again, there's that thing about habit. Sure, Kerry
enjoyed himself. But as the enjoyment palled, would
habit take over? Would the security of having some *one*
supplant the enjoyment of variety? God knows, you
could see them at any bar, the receding hairlines and

protruding bellies with no place else to go, waiting around for something to happen. One could assume that even an aging Kerry, in his ebullient Dutch-uncle way, could make something happen, but was that really the point? Was the point sheer enjoyment? Or what? Speculations like this led into all kinds of serpentine twists of thought that had no end to them.

If the questions led to puzzlement about Kerry, the same questions had some very clear answers with Scott, another steady at the bridge table. Scott was a hustler, a real no-nonsense professional who had it stashed away in the bank, and more going in all the time. He was tall, hefty, and nearly thirty, but he still had a boyish handsomeness, a wicked grin, and a zest for his work. He was reputed to be the best gay lay in New York.

When Scott came over for bridge, he'd leave my number with his answering service and the phone would suddenly come to frenetic life, with an astonishing variety of people at the other end of the line. One was a titan of the American arts who called while I was dummy, wanting Scott and some Seconals, too. Scott was playing the hand, and asked me to find out who it was. I found out and damn near dropped the phone. But Scott was at the business end of a three-no-trump. "Tell him to wait."

"*Him.* To wait?"

"He'll wait," said Scott serenely, and went into a string of spades.

He waited, by God.

Then there was the one out of the upper strata of Burke's Peerage. Scott had not yet arrived when this reedy voice over the phone announced that he was Lord Something-or-Other and he'd just gotten off the plane at Kennedy. He estimated that he would be through Customs and into the city within a couple of hours and wished to see Scott around teatime. I told him I figured that Scott would be heavy into the third rubber about that time and would a little later be suitable? Quite so. Seven would be entirely satisfactory. I hung up the phone with the exhilaration of having lived through one of life's experiences. Somehow I'd spent all my life missing out on arranging assignations between male hustlers and British lords. In fact, I felt the whole thing should have been dramatized by Gilbert and Sullivan.

But Scott was tactfully reticent about the scope of his contacts and only occasionally would he slip, as in a passing reference to "my shrink."

"Scott, a happy guy like you goes to a shrink?"

"Oh, no, honey. *My* shrink comes to *me.*"

When Scott wasn't being a call boy to his regular clientele, and was tired of the gentilities of the wealthy and wise, he'd go up to Fifty-third and Third and get right in there, like a flamingo among the chickens. "I made sixty dollars between four in the morning and six, today. Not bad, huh?" he said, airily, one time between rubbers, and went on to describe in some detail the ministrations he had given. His customers had undoubtedly gotten their money's worth, but it was difficult to concentrate on the bidding.

Scott might have five more good years as a hustler, and then what? He had capital, an engaging personality, and a vast knowledge of the gay scene. He also had financial sense and a gambler's instinct that showed up in his bridge bidding. He'd probably set himself up in some kind of business in a gay urban enclave, an enterprise that would involve a lot of contact with people, and go on to make a pile of money. His sex life would go on a volunteer basis and probably be as active as ever. Not bad. Scott probably had the least illusions of any of the gays who sat around that bridge table and his fine-honed sense of reality would stand him in good stead.

But I sensed another thing about Scott that he had in spades, that most other gays I knew had in hearts or diamonds. Scott was tough. Not in any leather-jacket machismo sense, not in the way that the chickens at the Stable Inn tried to be tough. He was in many ways a very gentle man, but there was a willow-switch resilience about him. He could bend, but he wouldn't break.

I remember reading, in the days of my closetude, about tragedies that seemed to circle around gays like buzzards. The incidents, well reported in the press, seemed to confirm the terrors of being caught, of coming out, of the basic emotional instability of gays. The reports could damp the soul with fear at the darkness within oneself. There, but for the Grace of God . . . All those psychiatrists are right: I *am* sick.

But seen from the other side of the closet door, the gay subculture looked very different. I mean, these babies were *tough!* Some gay could sit around the living-room table, recounting an emotional turmoil that might be expected to curl the hair of a straight (and certainly put a few curls in mine). The listeners would shake their heads at the end of the recital and one would shrug and say, "Oh, well, he'll get over it." And whoever "he" was probably would, with a little help from his friends.

But when you think about it, how could it be any other way? Tennessee Williams wrote in one of his short stories that whatever else may happen, sometimes a gay is going to have to go home alone. All alone. That specter of aloneness pervades gay literature, underlies the hope of finding someone to really care about, underscores the pathos of losing that cared-about someone. Yet in the long solitary walk home down the dark streets, the waking up to find an empty pillow beside you, the dark windows that confront you when you open the door at dinner time, all those moments in the practice of aloneness toughen the hide like leather, and spartan the spirit. Practice doesn't necessarily make perfect, but it helps. For the maturing gay, it is the basis for an emotional independence that most straights simply don't have.

The closest I ever came to falling completely apart had

nothing to do with my gayness. The trauma took place when my wife of many years took her leave, with more than ample reason, and left me . . . alone. The terrors of the next few days and nights were quite beyond anything I had ever lived through or ever expect to live through again. I was totally unpracticed in the arts and occasional pleasures of being alone. But it's a rare gay who isn't well practiced, and the older the gay, the tougher the hide.

It has to be.

Try it on for size. It's one o'clock in the morning and you've got to be at work at nine. You're bellied up at a gay bar after a night at the movies or theater, and beside you at the bar is this man—a nice-looking guy you dig. You go through the conversational openers and get a modest response and a winsome smile. Well and good. You find out that he's seen the same show you've seen and, on that basis, the conversation rambles on for a while. You're about ready to close in when he starts shifting from one leg to another, a curtain drops over his eyes, and he says he's got to meet a friend of his over at the Ninth Circle in ten minutes. And that's that. There's a guy on the other side of you at the bar, and a humpy number across the room. But some still small voice says to you that it is . . . one o'clock . . . in the morning . . . and the visions of that bed begin to look awfully good. No big deal. There's always tomorrow . . . and tomorrow is another day.

Congratulations; you've got a good hide. Better yet, you'll get up in the morning.

This resilient emotional toughness shows up in gentle form in the character of Dr. Daniel Hirsh in Penelope Gilliatt's script for the film *Sunday, Bloody Sunday*. The good gay doctor shares a bisexual artist—Bob—with a divorcee named Alex. Both Alex and the doctor settle for half a loaf, and when Bob decides to spend a few weeks in America, no loaf at all. At the conclusion of the film, with Bob already gone, Dr. Hirsh soliloquizes:

I want his company and people say, what's half a loaf, you're well shot of him; and I say, I know that, I miss him, that's all. They say he'd never make me happy and I say, I am happy, apart from missing him. . . . All my life I've been looking for someone courageous and resourceful, not like myself, and he's not it. But something. We were something.

I could almost hear Craig saying lines like that after his tempestuous split-up with Jesse. In the last analysis, "we were something," and that's to be kept, and stored away, and cherished, and if one is alone for a while, so be it. One survives, with a little help from one's friends. The telephone call, the casual visit, the gentle question, a bottle of wine, a bunch of flowers, a walk to the Morton Street pier. Contact. Kerry and Craig were expert at it, a kind of emotional pulse-taking. We all knew, almost day to day, the state of each other's psyches, who was currently involved with whom, and what shape the course of events was taking. Our awareness was very casual, like the purview of a lifeguard lolling on his high chair at the beach. The point was that the lifeguard was there, and if you got caught in an undertow, somebody would know about it and help you.

This kind of a mutual support system is, of course, prevalent in any group of close friends. Among straights, it's the girls at the beauty parlor or tennis club, the men at the golf club, or that New England institution, the town dump, or wherever. But among gays, the system seems particularly well developed because of the comparative lability of many gay relationships. Even the toughest hide can get wounded, and friends are there to staunch the wounds.

One evening, feeling out of sorts, I was down at a nefarious waterfront dive called Peter Rabbit. Like most other gay bars in the area, it had a distinctive clientele. Peter Rabbit's people were gays in their thirties and forties who had quite obviously been through much, but who had now found their snug harbor. They circulated around the bar area with greater assurance and less frenetic intensity than was evident at bars catering to a younger group. The music was more genteel, and the dancing—as might be appropriate in an establishment called Peter Rabbit—recalled the Bunny Hug.

I sat there, slouched in a corner, and observed the scene. Over by the cigarette machine stood a little man with a balding head, floppy ears, and a nose like a rabbit. He was probably at the fading end of his thirties, but you could see how somebody might have thought he was a pretty cute trick when he was twenty and had his hair. At any rate, he was just standing there alone, nursing his beer and staring at the floor.

The jukebox finished its chores in hard rock and lit into some sweepy-swoopy sentimental thing right out of the fifties, which inspired everybody on the dance floor to go into a touchy-feely thing, all misty-eyed with the remembrance of dear dead days at Cherry Grove. I slouched deeper in my chair, muttering "Aw, c'mon, fellows, pull yourselves together! Life goes on . . ." And then I noticed the rabbity man over by the cigarette machine. Two big tears were rolling down his cheeks and he pulled out a handkerchief. The old stereotype! The fading little queen, weeping her heart out for her lost youth at an end-of-the-line bar on the waterfront. A crummy cliché was standing there in the flesh.

Then something happened inside my head. I said to myself, if you can't emphathize with that crummy little queen, you'd better get your ass back to Baltimore and never mess with the gay scene again.

I stirred myself in the chair and slowly got to my feet. But I was too late. One of the older men at the bar had noticed him, crossed over, put an arm around his shoulder, and started talking to him gently. The little guy looked up and smiled.

It is doubtful that any such support, however fleeting, was given to the Hawk in the six months he spent in the Tombs. Yet what had happened to the Hawk was no spasm of beer-induced nostalgia, but the wrecking of his business and emotional life. The Hawk was a friend of Cory's, and at the time I first met him in the summer of 1971, he was one of the largest soft-drug dealers in Manhattan.

Cory and I went over to pay the Hawk a visit at his apartment. It was a strange place, filled with colored lamps. Two big black police dogs prowled in and out of the rooms. Seated in the living room was a youngster of seventeen or eighteen who was introduced as Steve. He had vague eyes. His mouth was petulant. But he was very good-looking, and he moved with a languid sexuality.

The Hawk himself was stocky and powerfully built. His face was molded strongly with a prominent nose. He spoke slowly. He moved slowly. He seldom smiled. There was a quietness about him reflected in his eyes. They looked at one directly, with little blinking, and they were thoughtful, ruminative, and not unkind. His voice was soft but reverberant. He looked as if he were in his mid-forties. I hadn't expected to like him (dope-dealers not being one of my particular enthusiasms in life) but I did. Strangely, I felt one could trust this man.

After the first meeting, he came over to the house a few times to visit Cory. One time he was tripping, and his movements and speech were even slower than usual. I'd also meet him on the street sometimes. He was always alone and plodded along in a businesslike way. And I'd hear about Steve from kids at the Stable Inn. Steve was known around there as the walking drugstore. "From Steve you can get absolutely anything," they'd say with awe. Then add: "Except skag. The Hawk's got a thing about skag."

I led them on. "But you can make a lot of money out of heroin."

The answer was firm. "The Hawk doesn't play with shit." Period.

The next thing I knew, I was reading about the Hawk in the papers. In a heavy-breathing account, the news story told of how the police had raided a village apartment and found over $750,000 worth of dope, including twenty pounds of what was evidently heroin. They gave the Hawk's real name and said that he had been taken into custody with bail set at $100,000. The story read like any other story of dope seizure, with the police portrayed as the relentless nemesis of Evil. But knowing the Hawk, it sounded strange. In the first place, I knew he never kept the stuff in his apartment. In the second place, what was he doing with all that heroin?

A few months later, I heard that they had picked up Steve on a drug bust, and deposited him on Rikers Island.

There the matter rested for several more months until one noon I answered the door, to find the Hawk standing there. He walked in with slow-moving dignity, and sat down. I put a cup of coffee in front of him, and he proceeded to talk for three hours. As each hour passed, I yearned more bitterly for a tape recorder. But there was none around, so I can only give a reconstruction from memory.

Steve had started out a couple of years before as one of the Hawk's runners, covering some of the West Village soda joints and other chicken roosts. The basic deal was 30 percent to the runner, 70 percent to the supplier. The basic commodities were grass, hash, mescaline, acid, and various types of ups and downs. Prices varied, with the dealer setting the price for that day and the runner either getting the price, reducing the price and taking it out of his own cut, or returning the unsold part of the day's supply.

The Hawk's part of the bargain is to get the merchandise in bulk (a ten cent pill, for instance, would retail for a dollar), make sure of its quality, store it, distribute it to the runners, and then keep track of them. His modes of acquiring the material to be sold were Byzantine, but the key to his success was to purchase—in cash—as large bulks as possible so that, while other dealers might run out of one drug or another at a given time, the Hawk— and the Hawk's runners—could always be relied upon for whatever the customer wanted. The Hawk had reached this capacity for bulk buying over the years without any financial angel. He lived very simply and plowed most of what he made back into the business. In effect, his life savings were in merchandise, and that merchandise was stored at an apartment on the Upper West Side in the care of an old man who lived there and for whom the Hawk paid the rent. The old man was, in effect, the caretaker of the warehousing operation. Whatever the Hawk needed, he went up to the West Side and got, or sent one of his trusted runners.

Trust was, of course, one of the keys to the operation. The Hawk had his ways of testing his runners, most of whom were in their late teens or early twenties and able to meld into the scene. Consignments were small at first, and quite a few potential runners would come back with some of the stock missing, or stoned out of their minds, or with the Hawk's share, but none of their own, or not come back at all. Testing runners was, to the Hawk, simply one of the risks of doing business—personnel training, if you will. He never resorted to rough stuff if a runner flaked out. The business relationship was simply severed.

Steve, the Hawk found, was meticulous. Night after night he not only came back with all his goods sold, plus the Hawk's 70 percent, but his own 30 percent as well, intact. Extracting just a bit for living expenses, he put the rest in the bank. The Hawk was mightily impressed. Here was a businessman after his own heart.

The Hawk was gay. Steve was beautiful. The Hawk felt

his emotional moorings giving way and began to look for some way to ease out of the relationship, or get further into it. As a usual practice, the Hawk kept the houseboys as both housekeepers and bedmates. When at that time one of the houseboys made his departure, the Hawk suggested that Steve take his place. He made the suggestion on the assumption that Steve would refuse and thereby give the Hawk an excuse to ease him out. But Steve didn't refuse; he moved right in.

What happened for the next six months or so was, from the Hawk's point of view at least (and probably from Steve's as well), a beautiful thing. A relationship at meridian or what you will, and each must have drawn an immense satisfaction from it. And then . . .

The Hawk, sitting there on the couch, rubbed his hand across his forehead and sighed. "Kids, you know, they go through stages. Steve, I could tell, was going into another stage. If I hung onto him, kept sleeping with him, kept him, you know, where he was—runner, houseboy, the rest—I don't know, maybe he'd have gone crazy, done something bad, maybe even killed me. You can't hold a kid like that back, when he's ready to go on. It didn't matter that I loved him . . . all that . . . he had to go on."

"How did you know?" I asked.

"You can tell. He tries to force it . . . to go back . . . to snuggle up and ask if you want anything . . . you know he's playing games . . . he doesn't mean it . . . he's just talking to himself. That's when it's important to give them a shove."

The Hawk got himself a new houseboy named Mike. But Steve continued to live in the apartment and work for the Hawk as a runner. Then things began to get complicated. Steve brought in an ex-lover named Randy. He also had a current lover. And the Hawk provided Mike, who was slightly built and carried large amounts of dope as part of his runner chores, with a bodyguard. All six of them lived at the Hawk's place.

Living arrangements like this might appear to border on the lunatic, but within the scene they are not unusual. The Hawk was a soft-hearted man and found it difficult to throw people out. So they just accumulated. But the household began to simmer with a lot of tensions, with each resident in some kind of dynamic relationship with each of the others.

Apart from doing his running tasks for the Hawk, Steve began spending more and more time with mob types who ran various of the gay bars and soda joints around town. The types made much of him and his friends and in the process learned a good deal about the operations of the Hawk. The bulk purchases. The cash. The West Side warehouse apartment. One evening, at one of the mobster's apartment, Steve got really stoned and spilled out the address of the warehouse.

Realizing what he had done, Steve and a friend of his went back to the Hawk and told him. Steve and the Hawk went up to the warehouse apartment and emptied it out, leaving the old man with his television set, and brought the dope down to the Hawk's own apartment, along with $5,000 in cash. Only Steve and the Hawk knew where the cash was hidden. But Randy knew that there was cash somewhere, and Randy at that time happened to be mad at the Hawk.

Events were closing in on Steve. He had sold out the Hawk by letting the mob types know where the bulk was. Then, in turn, he had sold out the mob types by tipping the Hawk off that the mob types might be raiding the warehouse. And then Randy, who had his own eye on the cash, moved in on Steve, pushing the idea that they had to neutralize the Hawk, and then get out of town until the mob types simmered down. For getting out of town they needed cash, right? You know where the cash is, Steve?

Right? If the Hawk isn't around, he's not going to worry about the cash, right?

The Hawk's voice was even, with no shade of hostility. "I don't know. Maybe it went something like that. Who knows what goes on in those kids' minds? And Steve, maybe he didn't know where he was at, with Randy pushing him, and all those mob types out there in the bushes."

While the Hawk was out shopping, Randy got a hold of the cash, went down to the precinct station and told the cops about the biggest stash of dope since the Opium Wars. The Hawk returned from the A & P. The cops got in a couple of squad cars and descended on the Hawk's place, seven or eight strong with plenty of artillery. Mike and the Hawk were in the apartment, putting the eggs and lettuce away in the refrigerator, when the cops burst in. It was a brilliant piece of law enforcement, except they didn't have a warrant. No matter. They hauled the Hawk, Mike, and three others away. They hauled the dope away. They hauled away a gun or two that they found in the apartment, and called a press conference. In addition to all the pills and grass and hash, they had in their possession this here white stuff which was going to be tested to find out if it was heroin. (The results of the tests came in several days later—lactose, which is used to cut cocaine. But the papers had forgotten all about the story by that time.)

The Hawk's bail was set at $100,000, which he was unable to raise. He and the four others spent six months in the Tombs awaiting trial and/or a reduction in bail. They finally got a reduction in bail. The case came up for a hearing and was thrown out on a technicality: no warrant. The Hawk and the four others were free. And completely broke.

The Hawk came back to his apartment to find the old man, one dog, and a lot of tunafish cans. Steve was in jail on a whole raft of present and past charges. Randy had sold out Steve, after the Hawk had been picked up, and tried to get away with all the money. By some strange happenstance, Randy died of an overdose.

Now the Hawk was here, sitting in the living room, slow-talking, sedate, his eyes meditative. "I got out of the Tombs about a week ago. Mike, the dog, the old man, they're all pretty much starving. I've got to get moving again. Been trying to figure out how to start—credit, all that."

"What do you think about Steve?" I asked.

He shrugged. "What's there to think?" His eyes seemed focused far away. "You've just got to go on, is all."

Chapter Ten

❧

Bruce. Shaggy-dog Bruce, boxer and everybody's pet chimp. After he and Cory had that big fight, and both of them had made their exit, each would come back periodically to touch base. Visiting hours tended to be around four in the morning. While Cory was likely to be stoned, Bruce was usually sober, all too coherent, and ready for an hour or two of genial and nostalgic conversation, which I was not ready for at all.

But sometimes Bruce showed up with someone else. I was grateful for that; at least it kept him occupied, balling his brains out on the couch. After Bruce went through his black drag-queen period, he brought in a few girls of truly startling ugliness. One of them gave him the clap, and he decided to go gay again. Not that a black drag-queen couldn't give him the clap just as easily as anyone else. It was the principle of the thing. If he went to all that effort to go straight, damnit, and conform to the accepted mores of the day, why should he be visited with the clap? Was someone trying to tell him something?

At any rate, Bruce went back to chickens again, and with his genius for acquiring people, the place began to look like a reviewing stand in a poultry yard. Such a cackle and flutter! And Bruce, bouncing up and down on the waterbed, crowing.

All the while, a strange thing was happening to Bruce. When he had first come around, he was very serious about his boxing. He made contact with a gym and worked out there almost daily. Periodically, he'd drag me up to some God-awful loft on Eighteenth Street to watch him work out his aggressions on a punching bag. He had a lot of aggressions. But in the course of his life in New York he slowly began to lose interest in boxing, and he finally quit altogether.

One evening when we were alone, I asked him about it. "It was the way it was, then," he said. "I was brought up with a pretty tough gang. You had to know how to use your fists, and I got better and better at it. Move in there fast, take care of two while everybody else was taking care of one. I figured maybe I had something. We used to go over to Reading and beat up people, black kids if we could find them, but there weren't too many. Old men, too. They were easy. And fags. We beat up a lot of fags, stole their wallets and ran. They never made any noise about it. Never went to the cops. It got so it was a big laugh. Get tanked up on beer and somebody would say, let's go over to Reading and have ourselves a fag. When we got his money, we'd have a lot more beer, and the bartender, he'd shake all our hands, congratulating us because we'd beaten up a fag." Bruce studied his fists as he went on talking. "One time, this guy, we got him around the corner from a gay bar. One guy held him from behind, and the other two of us went to work on him. Kneed him in the balls, punched him in the kidney, the belly. Then I got him square in the face. I could feel the bones give as I hit him. We dropped him, got his wallet, and the other two guys ran. I started to run, too, and then I stopped, went back to him. He was lying there, bleeding from the mouth and making funny sounds. I went around the corner to the gay bar, called an ambulance, went back and stayed with him. He opened his eyes and looked at me. Shit. Heavy. He could pick me out in a lineup later. But I wasn't thinking that. I don't know what I was thinking, except just that I had to wait with him till the ambulance came. I reached out and touched his hand, held it. Yeah. I held his hand. Then I heard the siren, and I ran. He was an older guy. He looked sort of like you."

As the months went by, poultry lost its savor for Bruce and the city did, too. He went back to his hometown in Pennsylvania where, he figured, his folks could get him a job. I heard nothing from him for six weeks or so, and then came the 4 A.M. knock at the door. In came Bruce, and behind him a girl, a real, live, and very attractive girl. He was quite breezy about the whole thing. "This is Rae. She's my wife."

"You're what?"

"Wife."

"You mean . . . married and all that?"

"Yup."

I turned to Rae. "What else can I say? Welcome!"

She grinned a great big beautiful grin and said, "Hi."

"How 'bout that?" said Bruce.

"You don't deserve it," said I, looked at her again, and said, "Wow."

Carlos peered out from the waterbed area. "What . . . in the name of God . . . is going on out there?"

I tried to explain the matter as calmly as possible. "Well, you see, it's this way. Bruce went and got himself married. . . ."

"Is he cute?" asked Carlos.

"He . . . is a her."

"You have got to be kidding."

"I am not kidding."

Carlos got on a bathrobe and came out to inspect the phenomenon.

Bruce gave him the big hello. Rae gave him the big hello. Carlos said, "In the middle of the night I should be confronted with . . . *this?*"

But there was no avoiding it. Rae, along with Bruce, was here for the weekend, and, as it turned out, a pretty fine time was had by all. For a small-town girl who had never been to the big city before, and landed in a nestful of gays, she kept a remarkable aplomb, even when Bruce took her down to Old Danny's to shoot a little pool. She shot a hard game and bellied up to the bar with the best of them. Bruce caused some initial consternation by introducing her around to all his old buddies, bedmates, and what-have-you, but once the initial shock wore off, she seemed to fit right in.

There was something about that girl. She was the quintessential tomboy, and bopping around Sheridan Square with Bruce, she was God's gift to unisex. Around the house, when Bruce would go into his playful chimp routine, she'd give as much as she took and, in moments of enthusiasm, pin him to the floor and sit on him. Carlos and I didn't quite know what to make of it. Said Carlos, with awe, "She's a better man than he is."

But not quite.

Carlos was then in his drag period and he kept eyeing Rae with appraising speculation. One evening he rummaged around in the back of the closet and came out with an evening dress right out of the thirties, one of those sylphlike things that Carole Lombard used to wear to display her charms to William Powell. Carlos handed it to Rae. "Put it on. I'm going to make a lady out of you."

Rae, sitting there in her denim pants and tee-shirt, stared at the garment as if it were from outer space. "What is it?"

"A dress."

"On me?"

"Go ahead."

Rae squared her shoulders. "All right, I will."

For the next half hour or so, while Bruce and I watched with growing amazement, Carlos proceeded to transform Rae into a truly beautiful woman. But as she sat there, with Carlos doing her hair, her knees were far apart as if she were still wearing pants. Her chin still jutted with playful belligerence. Then Carlos stood her up, and she looked at herself in the mirror. She looked at herself a long time, and when she turned to face us, she could have been the Duchess of Kent.

She pulsated with the magic of the feminine, and the three of us stared at her. Bruce was in awe. Carlos radiated empathy; he was both her and him looking at her as his artistic creation. My reactions were simpler: I was seized with spasms of raw lust. I sought to remind myself that I was, after all, a self-respecting gay and quite apart from that sort of thing. But the reminder did no good whatsoever. I had a very heavy thing about that girl. Bruce obviously had a heavy thing about her, too. And Carlos? Well, he was not unimpressed. Who was this Rae, anyway?

She was no fag-hag in any sense that I understand the phrase. She didn't radiate any of the motherliness that would attract the more fragile of the brethren. She came on direct, four-square, and no-nonsense, yet there was a rib-nudging playfulness about her that resonated as everybody's happy kid sister. You could just see her out there in left field, her baseball cap askew, yelling at the umpire, but you knew that in a pinch she could take over first base and do a good job of it. She was ineffably one of the boys, and, at the same time, she was ineffably feminine. The prismatic changes she could go through in the course of a day were dazzling.

Some of those changes were in a minor key. One time, after Rae and Bruce had made several visits to New York, she and I were alone for an afternoon. Carlos was at his studio, and Bruce was . . . somewhere. She sat on the couch and stared into space. "How did I get myself into all this?"

"All what?"

"Where's Bruce?"

"Around."

"That's what I mean. Off with some queen? How do I know?"

"What did you know when you married him?"

"That he'd been playing around in the gay scene down here in New York. He told me that."

"What else did he tell you?"

"That he didn't do much of anything. Just played around."

"Do you believe that?"

"I don't know what to believe."

"Does it matter?"

"Yes, it matters."

"What? That he did a lot more than play around, or that he's lying to you?"

"Both." She paused. "I told him that if I found out he'd done anything more than play around, I'd leave him." Another pause. "Maybe I shouldn't have said that."

"Right. You shouldn't. You'll just keep him lying to you."

There was fire in her eye. "Then why did he want to get tied in with me? If he's got all these . . . people down here. Why me?"

"Because you're you."

"And who's that? I'm just me." Pause. "And all I want is a nice straight husband!"

"Maybe you'll find him. But I'll give you odds you won't."

"Why not?"

"Because . . . because . . . " I floundered around. "Because you vibe with us."

"How do you mean?"

I floundered some more. "Look . . . you like it here?"

"Sure."

"You feel comfortable here?"

"Sure."

"You like the people?"

"Sure."

"And we like you. You fit. I don't know how that is, but it is, and we know it."

"You mean I'm going to spend my life hung up with a bunch of gays?"

"Bisexuals, please. You're the 'bi' in us."

"I don't think I like that." She frowned. "But I like it here." She frowned harder. "But . . . *Damnit!*"

The next time Bruce showed up, it was not with Rae, but with some straight young man. Bruce said he had left Rae because . . . well, they'd had this argument about the scene . . . and he was going to Arizona with the straight-arrow. They were leaving the East forever to homestead among the Indians or something.

The straight-arrow turned out to be less than straight. He and Bruce got into this threesome on the hideabed with one of the local talents. Bruce did his thing in ten minutes. Straight-arrow took it from there with the local talent for the rest of the night while Bruce just lay there in the nether reaches of exasperation. The next morning they left for Arizona. It was evident that the straight-arrow, having made his new discovery, had every intention of laying waste to the countryside from here to the last and ultimate Grand Canyon.

I kept thinking about Rae.

I kept thinking about laying it on the line, or not laying it on the line. What seemed apparent was that Bruce had at least given it a try, not only by telling her about his life in the scene in New York, but by bringing her right into the midst of it. Okay, she had conceded that point, but she couldn't concede to herself that he could really have been a part of it. And because she couldn't, he couldn't. All of which left them hanging in a spider web of questions, implicit and unanswered. Or asked and less than answered.

Rae's reactions were well understandable. She could accept the idea that Bruce, before meeting her, had sown his wild oats. But *these* wild oats? And just how long was it going to go on? And was she, through Bruce, going to be "hung up on a bunch of gays" for the rest of her life?

But the puzzlement was Rae herself, the particular equations of her personality that had brought Bruce to her in the first place and that made her a delightful and easygoing sometime member of this household. Something in her was beautifully adapted to something in us. Yet something in her insisted that she couldn't cope. So Bruce had left for Arizona.

I kept fretting about that, and the disquiet lay no less in the knowledge that there wasn't one damn thing I could do about it. Still . . . the speculations kept going around in my head.

Rae was, by all signs that I saw of her, a man's woman. Well, then, was there such a thing as a gay man's woman? Questions like that evoked images of Mae West and her musclemen, or Tallulah Bankhead and her choiring angels. But Rae had no similarity whatever to Mae West or Tallulah Bankhead! Nor did she seem to bear any resemblance to fag-hags like Linda, whom I had first met over at Cory's on Bayard Street. To Linda, it seemed to me, gay companionship was a snug harbor from the storms of hooking; she was there for gentle and disinterested companionship. She reached across into another state of being. But not Rae. She was no alien. She fitted. Yet she fitted as herself, without any mask, or pretense, or act. Linda and all those Hollywood types seemed like out-landers. Rae seemed like part of the culture. Where the hell did that leave things? Clinical impressions were leading to considerable confusions. About the best I could come up with was that Rae was, indeed, "the 'bi' in us," and her presence could stir it. Beyond that . . . what we were to her, what the equation was between us . . . nothing more than a glimmering.

Then I had this weird thought about the women who had really meant something to me in my life. They had set the theme of which Rae was simply a variation. They were gutsy, no-nonsense women with a sense of identity and an independence that came of that sense. They could deal across the board; they could make decisions; they could move; and they could go. None of them had much use for the fluttering wiles or cloying self-pity in-volved in the conventional concepts of femininity. Yet they had sensitivity, awareness, a capacity for caring and conserving.

The line of thought got heavier and heavier. If any of those women had been male, she could have been the best of the gays. In their range of emotional conscious-ness, they were full-dimension people, just as, say, Ver-non or Craig were full-dimension people. They could run the gamut of those characteristics that are called "masculine" and those that are called "feminine." The variety of roles they could play was almost infinite, rang-ing free of the rigidities of gender-bound self.

Then reverse it. Suppose all the men mentioned in this book had, in fact, been women. A speculation like that is surely enough to boggle the mind! Carlos, for instance, and his feminine alter-ego, Monique. What if it had been the other way around and I'd been shacked up with this beautiful Peruvian girl named Monique? One fine night she confesses to me that she's got this alter-ego named Carlos and she has this deep urge to dress up like a man and be Carlos. Would it really make all that much difference? After all, I could tell the dear girl that some of my best friends were men, and if she wanted to dress up and be a man, right on! Monique-Carlos would still be as full-dimensional (and really the same person) as Carlos-Monique, with the same admixture of qualities. So it might be with Cory, or Lamont, or Kerry, or Vernon, or Bruce. Bruce? The boxer? Even Bruce?

I once met a guy like Bruce when I was fairly sloshed at one of the waterfront bars. The more beer I took, the better he looked. The more beer he took, the sleepier he got. And I decided that the one big project I had for that evening was to get that number home. We talked for a long while in a drowsy beer-soaked way. He had a pushed-in face, a cute sidewise grin, close-cropped hair, and an amiable fatality about life that I assumed must have developed in gangfights in the South Bronx. Rough trade, sure, but there was a gentleness about him.

Arms around each other, we wove our way up Christopher Street, steadying the trees and lamp posts as we went. We sang a little, sighed a lot, and exchanged incoherent profundities. Several passers-by emanated evil vibes and he swore to beat the shit out of them, but the passers-by passed by in the night and so did his aggressions. We arrived at my apartment—barely. I steered him to the bed. He collapsed, sprawling, a slim, muscular body that in my addled head was beautiful to behold.

You guessed it. There are girls like Bruce, and they have their charms. That girl was truly full-dimensional. None of the conventional words—dyke, fag-hag, or what-you-will—applied. None of the conventional concepts of transvestism applied. That girl, like Rae, inhabited a crossroads ground, neither here nor there, but everywhere, a crossroads ground of gender that was home turf to gays as well. Why was the relationship so empathic, the recognition so clear? Maybe because we all lived in the same neighborhood. Or, in another metaphor, maybe we were, like Carlos and Monique, two sides of the same coin.

About a month after Bruce had left for Arizona with the not-so-straight-arrow, I called Rae at her family's place in Pennsylvania to find out what was going on. But Rae, it seemed, wasn't living with her folks anymore. Where was she living? Oh, she had this apartment with Bruce. Oh, Bruce was back? Oh, yes. Well, have them give me a ring sometime.

A half-hour later, the phone rang. Three days later, at the usual 4 A.M. (it was a five-hour hitch from their hometown), there was a knock at the door. In they trooped, the two of them, happy Jacks as ever. Bruce, it seemed, had gotten as far as Virginia in his hegira to Arizona. Rae, in the meantime, had had a chance to think things over. Bruce turned around and hitched back to Pennsylvania. He'd got a job as a recreation worker. She had a job waiting on table in a restaurant. They found an apartment. And that—for the time—was that. Somehow, I felt a glow for them.

But the melody lingered on. The next morning, Bruce, looking around at the various and sundries who happen to have crashed there the night before, started going on about the great and glorious freedoms of life in the Village. Rae sat there and listened with hooded eyes. "If you miss it," she said, "you can always go back to it. Nobody's stopping you."

Choice. I couldn't blame Rae for thinking that way. She'd come a long way already. How could I say that it wasn't a choice, but a continuum? She and we were all at the crossroads together and Bruce loved her because she was at the crossroads. He had married his psychic neighbor.

There is an old saw about gays: Question—Would you want your son to marry one? Answer—I don't know about that, but I certainly wouldn't want my daughter to marry one. Ostensibly, very good sense. The anguish of women married to closet cases is all too real—the puzzlement about that mysterious x factor in their husbands that exerts an unpredictable gravitational pull. A woman married to a closet case can never know her whole husband, can never fully map the territories of his emotional life. There is always that other something, lurking out there. . . .

But Rae? She certainly knew the territory. As well as the names and numbers of some of the players. There was no sinister mystery about it, and if she had to cross the bedroom area to go to the john while Carlos and I happened to be making love, so be it. She could even give a fair answer to that whispered womanly question: "What do men *do* together?" So, her husband had done it. Her husband might do it again. Troubling it might be, but mysterious it was not.

I had certainly been nonplused when Bruce had first shown up with Rae, but as time went on I began to think that Bruce, for whatever reason or instinct, had done the right thing in bringing her into his old life. She could never go into dark speculations about "those people he used to know in New York." She knew their names, faces, personalities, and habitats and, for the most part, she liked them. But her affinity for us proceeded from the fact that Rae herself had an awareness, vague or not so vague, that she, too, was a native of the crossroads.

Perhaps there is a counterquestion to that old saw about "marrying one": What's your daughter like? I could imagine any number of women who should not, under any circumstances, be married to Bruce or any other gay I knew. But Rae was not one of them. Rae, once she knew the territory, could handle it, and, I had a hunch, empathize with it.

So what was in the cards for Rae and Bruce? How
would Rae, knowing that Bruce was at least partly gay,
handle the situation? It was a fair assumption that Bruce
would, in the course of their marriage, get involved in an
occasional gay episode. Rae, being alert to the situation,
would probably know about it, or at least make a few
educated guesses. Then what? She could ignore it. She
could use her considerable charms to reel him back in.
Or she could make a grand stand.

She had already made her first grand stand, and that
hadn't worked. Considering the component of gayness
in Bruce, it probably wouldn't work in the future either.
The urge in Bruce would, on occasion, simply be too
strong for him to suppress. But assuming there would be
episodes, the key objective would be to keep them just
that—episodes—and not let the power of a gay relationship take hold of Bruce. Rae had a lot going for her. She
had, for one thing, the law and the prophets on her side:
she was married to him, and Bruce had enough of the
conventional in him to take that with some seriousness.
He had a kind of institutional loyalty to the idea of having
a wife. That really *proves* I'm straight! Which, of course,
is a pardonable overstatement, but still the legality of
marriage conferred a certain reassurance.

Rae also had a knowledge of her man. Not just his
gayness, but his satisfactions, his enthusiasms, his
rhythms of interest and boredom, and his emotional dimensions. She knew what turned him on and what
turned him off far better than any casual trick that Bruce
might find in the underbrush. She could conjure up diversions, when diversions were called for, excursions
and blandishments to catch his eye and interest.

She could also have it out with him, and probably
would on more than one occasion, not in the sense of
making a grand stand but simply: "I know what's going
on. Want to talk about it?" A bald question like that to
a closet case would probably shatter the household for

months, but Bruce, on the other hand, might just want to get it off his chest, and feel at ease in doing so.

In a way it all sounds very familiar. The wandering husband is not unknown to the straight culture. Legalities, diversions, and talk-fests are all part of the literature. But there are some differences here. Rae doesn't need to think that "the other woman" is somehow smarter, or sexier, or younger, or more exciting than she is. There is no "other woman," and no assault on her identity as a woman. Bruce just has this thing about men, and that's a very different ball game. It's an issue with him, not with her. Sure, the situation might be emotionally jarring, but it wouldn't have that special anguish that relates to her own womanhood.

Given Rae as Rae, and Bruce as Bruce, I had a hunch they stood a better chance of making it than a good many straight couples I knew. They were at least aware of their situation and could act on that awareness. But beyond that was the curious compatibility that came of similarities of temperament rather than the disparities of rigid sex roles in many straight relationships. Their relationship was a lot more fluid, and hence might be able to fill larger dimensions of each one's needs. But this optimism applies to the particular circumstances of Rae and Bruce.

I could imagine situations where a marriage with a lavender streak running through it could be an unholy mess, and the casebooks are probably full of them. The question is not why so many of them fail, but why some of them succeed. Bruce and Rae were just one inconclusive example of how such a marriage might provide the fulfillment that each partner needed and wanted. But central to that example is one clear tenet of Gay Liberation. Bruce's gayness was out on the table, understood and acknowledged both by himself and his wife. Their marriage, like a lot of others, might have many surprises, but there was no time-bomb ticking away in the closet.

Chapter Eleven

✖

One evening, in a fit of cultural evangelism, I took one of the brighter of the Stable Inn flock to see Peter Brook's film of *King Lear* starring Paul Scofield. It was a pretty gruesome piece of work—all winter settings in harsh black and white, heavy fur-draped wagons being dragged over the tundra from one armed encampment to another as Lear did his addled thing with his daughters. But at one moment, Scofield and the film came to life as the old man pleaded, "Let me not be mad."

The kid came out of the movie shaking his head. "How come they made a whole movie about that crazy old man?" The entire project was incomprehensible to him. What's an old man to do, except die as inconspicuously as possible? In fact, why wasn't he dead already?

A good many of the gays I knew were reasonably well convinced that they were going to die by the age of thirty-five. Beyond that was only a long drift of years as a "tired old queen" or a "doddering old troll." Most of them would rather not be bothered with so somber an ending to a gay life. Better to just get out before the gloom set in. "Let me not be mad." Or ugly. Or pouchy. Or wrinkled. Let me just . . . go.

They'd sit around the living room talking like this in perfect seriousness, while I sat there, shaking my head in bemusement. Because, while all the goings-on that this book relates were going on, I was in my early fifties—an age generally believed to be about a decade younger than God. But the actuarial expectancy of those young things sitting around the living room was a full seventy years. I said as much one evening and the chill in the room was palpable. "Seventy years? What am I going to do for . . . seventy years? My God, what am I going to look like when I'm seventy?"

The panic of confronting seventy years was, to anyone in middle age, sort of amusing. But the panic was real enough, and anything but amusing to the young gays confronting it. The prospect was something they hadn't the foggiest idea how to handle, and they had very few models to offer them any assurance whatever that life beyond thirty or so was anything but a trash bin. What older gays, after all, did they see? Under what circumstances? Hustlers see their Johns under those furtive and impersonal arrangements of trade that preclude much communication. Hearing hustlers talk among themselves gives the general impression that about all they know about Johns are their paying habits and their sundry and unusual sexual appetites. You rarely if ever hear a hustler start a sentence with "This John said to me" but plenty of sentences begin, "Hey, you know what this crazy old coot wanted me to do to him last night?" Of course that "crazy old coot" might be a professor of history, vice president of a bank, or a world-traveled diplomat, but you'd never know it from the hustler. Most likely, he wouldn't know it himself—or care. Why should he? He has no expectancy that that professor is going to tell him bedside stories about the Norman Conquest. All he knows is that the guy has hairy shoulders and likes to fuck sideways, and he pays twenty.

The street queens did a little better. One I knew spent months working his way through the NYU faculty. It was geology one night, chemistry the next, and English literature for two nights running. He got quite a groove out of it. "They even *talk* to me once in a while! Of course, I don't know what the hell they're talking about, but it's nice to hear them talk." Too bad. With concentration he might have gone through all the freshman survey courses in the school!

Then, the bars. But the bars usually didn't offer much opportunity for younger gays to see older gays in operation. The bars I knew were fairly well stratified, and each appealed to a distinctive crowd of related occupations, sexual tastes, life-style, and age. At places like the Ninth Circle and Dancing Danny's it was a rare night when you found many people over thirty, or with hair much less than shoulder-length. There were plenty of other bars where it was difficult to find someone under thirty. Where there was a generational mix, as, for instance, at Old Danny's, it was a rare older gay whom any youngster would want to use as a model for anything. They were likely to be closet cases from uptown or New Jersey who were sloshed and on the make.

In his book *The Washington Pay-Off*, Robert Winter-Berger relates how, in his role as Washington lobbyist and factotum, he was once called upon to get a U.S. senator out of the clutches of the police following a raid on one of the Village gay bars.

Looking at this incident from the vantage point of 1964 when it took place, one could see it as just another juicy scandal right out of an Allen Drury novel. But in post-liberation 1972, speculations do arise. For instance, wouldn't some of the people at that bar have been enriched by knowing a man of the senator's considerable stature in American political life? And wouldn't the senator's perceptions perhaps have been broadened, and his awareness enhanced, if he had known some of those people he sat shoulder-to-shoulder with at the bar as other than winsome young things? And one can go on to wonder just what the senator has found it in his heart to say publicly about gay rights, particularly in such areas as federal employment.

There were, of course, a few public figures who had made notable successes in life and who were known and self-acknowledged as gays. Tennessee Williams. W. H. Auden. Merle Miller. Paul Goodman. But most of them had very special talents in the arts. Very few gays are at all visible in government, the professions, business, sports, the labor movement, religion, or education. Because of their invisibility, younger gays who might have vocational inclinations or talents in those directions cannot point to this man or that one and say: He was a gay and he made it, I can make it too. Or: That guy didn't die at thirty-five. He went on and did what he wanted to do, and he isn't leading such a bad life at forty or fifty, or whatever.

I have a feeling that a lot of the talk about who is and who isn't in publicly visible positions is not just a reassurance exercise of the we-are-not-alone variety, but also an attempt to establish lines of identification with mature achievement. Like any other group of young people, young gays need that sense of identification. They don't get it because their models are locked in the closet. One of the ramifications of wider public acceptance of the facts of life as far as gay prevalence is concerned is that younger gays will have a lot more visible models to see and pattern their lives after. Perhaps fewer kids will be knocking their heads against the wall trying to get into such visibly gay vocations as the theater and interior decoration, for which they may not have any talent whatever.

About the only way that a younger gay can get a full-dimensional view and understanding of a mature gay in operation is to live with him. In large urban centers, this is not an uncommon practice and, as this book indicates, it has both its turmoils and its charms. Perhaps it all comes down to Carlos' parting shot: "Thank you, Wallace, you run the best finishing school in New York."

Lamont, late of Ethiopia via Athens, Georgia, was a product of various "finishing schools" in the gay subculture and they did pretty well by him. He was, in the course of time, even persuaded to abandon his petty ripoffs. Vernon, to a lesser extent, was another example.

But it was a different case with kids in their late teens who had lost their moorings with their families, usually because the families had found out they were gay and, to varying degrees, had broken contact with them. Sometimes the break was explosive. Sometimes it was just a slow-settling chill. Sometimes, in fact, it was the youngster himself who made the break, finding it harder and harder to relate to his family. But whatever the mode of cleavage, the family ceased to be the prime referent of authority. In transferring over into the gay subculture, it was difficult to find a surrogate.

Yet these young gays needed someone, not in the sense that a child needs an encompassing family, but in the sense that a maturing adult needs a guide and an emotional home base. The gay subculture does not have a clear surrogacy mechanism or institutional practice to take the family's place. There is no gay "next-of-kin."

Which led to all sorts of strange situations around here, especially with the cops. Let's say one of the tribe would go out some fine evening and get himself busted on a minor charge. Around 2 A.M. I could expect to get a phone call from a gruff cop at one of the local precinct houses. Since at that hour I tend to be pretty gruff myself, we'd go through some hard Raymond Chandler dialogue to establish the fact that he was a cop and I was . . . well, somebody whose name and phone number the kid had given him. At any rate, the kid was being held on such and such a charge at such and such a precinct, and . . . pause . . . who was I? Family? A lawyer? No. A friend? Call it that. If the cop was a smart cop—and many of them were—there'd be a pause and a shift of gears at the other end of the phone. When he started talking again, he'd be talking as if I were the kid's family and we'd go on from there.

Sometimes the gay and straight cultures get entangled in a situation. One of the tribe was an archetypal dizzy queen named Edwin, who, in his drag identity, was known as Wina. Edwin had spent a number of years in one of the state hospitals in almost total withdrawal. But when he came out, he came out manic. I never could be sure how much was a camp act (and he could be hilarious at times), and how much was a manifest of his mental illness. I tended to think that most of it was an act—a preening mechanism to attract the numbers. And attract attention he did. At the Ninth Circle or Danny's he and a couple of other queens would go through a long Marie Dressler–Wallace Beery routine right out of *Tugboat Annie* that nobody had seen the likes of in a while! Edwin and his sisters would hang in the bars till 4 A.M. (closing time), then proceed to a local hash house till six or so, and finally either pick up a trick or crash at some other queen's house to sleep and start the whole process over again, beginning at four or so in the afternoon. It was gay herding in extremis. The hardy types survived it. But Edwin was not hardy.

One evening Edwin swept into the apartment, went

through Garbo, Bette Davis, Diana Ross, a short run-down on news along the Rialto, a discourse on clothes, Marilyn Monroe, an autobiographical fragment from his sixth year, and an account of his mother's breakup with her second husband—all in about fifteen minutes. It was, even for Edwin, an appalling performance.

But underneath the obbligato of his talk, I sensed a slow beat of desperation. When he said, "Have a heart!" was he playing Joan Blondell, or Edwin? When he said, "I can't go on like this!" was it a Bette Davis line, or his? The identities were strewn all over the room, but some-where in that room was Edwin, and Edwin was giving a Macedonian cry. The problem was, I couldn't find Ed-win. It was like looking for a live body in a warehouse filled with manikins.

Edwin swept out into the night for his rounds of the bars. The next morning I got a call from one of the psychiatric clinics in town, asking if I knew Edwin, and notifying me that he had turned himself in for observa-tion. A week or so later I got a call from Edwin's mother out in Queens. The people at the clinic had asked her to take him back, but she couldn't take him back because she couldn't handle him in his manic state. Could I take him? I had a full house at that time, and couldn't, and suggested to her that he was probably better off at the hospital than squirreling around the Village bars. She said she'd keep in touch, and that was that, for six hours. At which point, Edwin showed up on my doorstep, hav-ing flown the coop at the clinic. He was in the middle of an Ingrid Bergman thing from Casablanca when the phone rang. Edwin's mother informed me that Edwin had escaped from the clinic, and she expected the men with the fishnets to be around at any moment. Did I know where he was? I did a tender-tough Bogart thing with Ingrid, and put him on the phone with his mother. They went on for a while about how he should get the hell back to the clinic. When Edwin and his mother hung up, I told him he should go back to the clinic, and keep taking his medication. Edwin considered the matter, went out, and spent the night getting gloriously drunk in every gay bar south of Fourteenth Street. In the morning he went back to the clinic. His mother called that day to tell me everything was under control.

A week later I got a call from Edwin's psychiatrist at the clinic. In the event that Edwin's discharge is indicated, he thought it would be a good idea if I came to a conference along with his mother. So now I'm sitting here trying to visualize what this conference is going to be like with Edwin's mother, Edwin's psychiatrist, and me, sitting around trying to figure out what to do with Edwin.

Purely medical problems were not quite so bizarre. And may the Lord bless the Lowenstein Clinic at St. Vincent's Hospital, the Northern Dispensary, and the city West Side VD clinic! The tribe needed them all. If it wasn't the clap, it was trench mouth. If it wasn't trench mouth, it was a sore on the foot, an ache in the belly, a cold in the head. They'd come wandering in here with a bewildered expression of what do I do now? Considering the regimen that some of those kids were on, sometimes speeding for days at a time, it's a wonder they didn't come down with the plague. Some of them would drift in, crash, and sleep for twenty-four hours straight. They'd wake up, looking like pole-axed sheep, revive themselves partially with an orange soda, and stare at the wall for another two hours. Then they'd drift over to the desk where I'd be working. I'd feel a hand on my shoulder, and hear a far-off voice saying, "Hey, I got this problem . . ." Which could be almost anything, and might be serious. At any rate, I was somebody who would listen and might have some ideas or suggestions. Mostly, somebody gave a damn, and had enough experience to be able to push a few buttons or turn a few dials in the mysterious mechanisms of the dominant culture.

One time, however, under the press of what seemed like emergency circumstances, I was taken into a very different culture. A sometime resident was a Japanese who had a name of oriental inscrutability but who liked to be called "Sam." He looked like Madame Butterfly, had the body of a Ming vase, and the personality of Ghengis Khan. He was one of the few gays I knew who seemed genuinely unhappy about being gay. I had the feeling that, if he had had his druthers, he'd have been galloping all over seventeenth-century Japan lopping off heads in the proud samurai tradition. The image was improbable, since Sam weighed less than a hundred pounds and had a delicacy about his person that evoked an exquisite flower arrangement.

One evening Sam worked himself into a fierce samurai mood of resoundingly hetero dimensions, went out, and bought himself a big black cigar. Upon returning, he retired to the waterbed and in a few moments clouds of smoke emerged and the apartment was filled with a stench of truly appalling acridness. After opening a window, I went in to find Sam, stark naked, propped up on a bunch of pillows, puffing away. I'd have as soon seen Madame Butterfly walk onto the stage of the Metropolitan Opera in a Baltimore Colt's football helmet. Still, moods are moods, and if Sam wanted to work his way through a Kurosawa movie that evening, it was nothing that a few hours' air-conditioning couldn't cure.

But shortly thereafter, sounds emerged from the waterbed area, sounds that indicated either Sam was watching a rerun of *Ugetsu* on television or was about to commit hara-kiri. I went in to find that my beloved Yellow Peril had turned green. The cigar was still smoldering away in the ashtray, but Sam, his eyes half closed, looked as if he were undergoing pulmonary convulsions. I grabbed him and held him, pounding his back. Then I got him to his feet. His eyes opened, and he gasped, "Black cloth. Get a black cloth!" and collapsed again. I had a dark blue suitcuff in the bureau drawer.

"Okay, what do I do with it?" I asked.

"Light it," he said. "Evil spirits."

I was about to declare that American Medical Science Does Not Recognize Any Role of Evil Spirits in the Etiology of Disease when Sam sprawled at the foot of the bed and went into another spasm.

I lit the damn cloth.

"Wave it over me," he commanded.

I waved it. It smelt almost as bad as the cigar.

"Say—'Evil spirts, leave the body.'"

"Aw, shit," I said.

Sam had another spasm.

I said, "Evil spirits, leave the body."

"Keep saying it," he gasped.

Bidding farewell to the last faded remnants of reason and dignity, I waved the cloth some more and chanted, "Evil spirits, leave the body."

I guess they did. At any rate, he was okay in another hour, and I never did find out whether the evil spirits were in the cigar or the memory of all those butch samurai.

I haven't been called upon for acupuncture yet, thank God.

Jobs were a constant problem. Cory had pioneered a job as a messenger for a record distribution company. When he left it, the job passed on to Vernon, who kept it for a while and then passed it on to another gay, who goofed it up by going on a two-day acid trip. Which fouled up that source. Certain hash houses and gay bars in the Village made it a regular practice to hire young gays. One of the dowager queens over in Brooklyn had a wide-ranging collection of contacts that usually led to employment of some sort. (The agency fee was customarily paid in bed.) But to hold down a regular, no-nonsense, meat-and-potatoes kind of job in an office or a factory or retail operation, young gays had to make a lot of adjustments. They had to work with straights, for one thing. That usually meant going back into the closet —or getting razzed, or slugged, or fired (probably all three). In addition, ordinary countercultural compromises were required, like wearing shoes and cutting one's hair. Plus specifically gay variations, like taking the butterfly patches off the seat of one's pants.

But there were subtler problems. In addition to the countercultural disquiet with much of any kind of organized work as a sellout to the powers and principalities and a corrosion of spontaneity and individuality (Love them? Yes. But a hand, like Tevye's, to Heaven!), there was the added complication of young gays' relationship with older men. Think back, for a moment, to Carlos and the struggle he had with all that flattery and ego-inflation poured onto him by older gays for their own purposes. His was a struggle to get his head back together and in touch with reality. Older men to Carlos meant, preeminently, one thing, and he played with them one role— and it wasn't an employer-employee relationship! As time went on, of course, one could expect that his emergent sense of reality would encompass such a relationship, but it would be slow in coming.

What was true of Carlos was, to a lesser extent, true of a lot of other young gays. The idea of working with older straight men in a single-purpose functional relationship that had nothing to do with sex was puzzling. For the most part, it wasn't part of their experience. Teachers, yes, but bosses, no. Through long and titilating speculations as to whether or not the boss was gay, or could be had, they'd try to get the situation changed around to where they could understand and operate within the context. The work part of it? Well, that was just how you made money. A sense of vocation was very hard to find.

As of now, transgenerational contacts among gays are severely limited, even more so than among straights, by the social repression of homosexuality. Older gays in established positions and with a record of achievement usually don't want to jeopardize their careers by identifying themselves as gay. Hence they avoid keeping some younger gay around the house, or even maintaining steady contact with him. But if the younger gay has been cut off, to a greater or lesser degree, from his own family, where does that leave him? Where are his moorings? Where are the transgenerational responsibilities that are still prevalent and accepted in the straight world?

Turn the question around. Most thoroughgoing homosexuals never marry and never have children. As they mature, where are their transgenerational linkages? I mean, *linkages*, relationships that are more than a happy evening with a number from a local gay bar, or surreptitious Thursday nights. It is quite possible that they could be as enriched by such relationships as younger gays.

Let's go back to that movie *Sunday, Bloody Sunday*, because it bears on this problem. The triangle involves Bob, a young designer-artist in his twenties who oscillates between Alex, a divorcee in her thirties, and Daniel Hirsch, a physician who is perhaps in his late forties or early fifties. The relationships are sketched with drypoint neatness and authority. With Alex, Bob is playful, affectionate, with, every so often, a touch of small-boy petulance. With Daniel, he is also affectionate, but there is a kind of seriousness about it that doesn't seem to relate to the depth of emotion but to the difference of the linkage. Daniel is older, has professional stature, and an internal dignity that elicits both respect and dependence.

When Bob holds Alex, he holds joyous sexuality. But when he holds Daniel, he holds security. And he needs them both.

In the course of the film Bob decides to go to America for a visit, leaving both Daniel and Alex. One of the key speculations of the film is the nature of that visit. Bob assures Daniel that it won't be for long. "I couldn't ever just piss off, you see," he says, but in a comment just after that line in the screenplay, the writer, Penelope Gilliatt, notes that "Bob could almost certainly do just that."

Daniel asks, "America would be for much longer than you say, wouldn't it?"

"I don't know," says Bob. "I'll have to play it by ear when I get there."

The clear implication of the film's ending is that Bob's playing it by ear will lead to his staying permanently in America. He will, indeed, "just piss off," leaving Alex and Daniel bereft.

Maybe the "Bobs" Mrs. Gilliatt knows are different from the "Bobs" I know. But I caught myself muttering toward the end of the film, Oh, for heaven's sake, dear people, relax! The kid will be back in three weeks and you'll all be in the soup again. So take a breather, you need it.

I simply could not accept the film as the emotional tragedy that I guess it was supposed to be, because in what was ostensibly a rather eccentric living arrangement, Bob had it made. His life was in a beautiful emotional balance. Once he got to America and played it by ear for a couple of weeks, he'd realize it and go running back to London to get both the joy and the security he needed, and put both Alex and Daniel on tenterhooks again. So it goes.

The script of *Sunday, Bloody Sunday* is an excellent piece of work, but it is written with a definite point of view. Bob is a sex-object being pursued by two people who are emotionally dependent on him. Well and good. But Bob wouldn't have gotten himself into that situation if he hadn't done some pursuing himself. For instance, take the scene in which Daniel is hosting a collection of drunken friends one evening when Bob walks in, hangs around awhile, and starts to leave. Daniel is the suppliant. "Go upstairs. I'll get rid of them. I'll come up as soon as I can." And when Bob refuses, Daniel, both angry and anguished, points to the door and says, "O.K. Off." Typical. Typical. Typical. I'll never remember the number of times I've made a grand gesture to the door and, in basso profundo, said, "All right . . . *out!*" when the one thing I wanted most in the world was for him to stay.

But one can imagine scenes that are not in the movie, as when Bob might have shown up at Daniel's at a time when Daniel, preoccupied with some professional task, would just as soon not have Bob around, when he'd want to say "O.K. Off," and mean it. Bob, with his own modes of blandishment, would stall off the exit, because at that moment he really needed Daniel. Such things happen. It would be as substantial a part of their relationship as any pursuit that Daniel might make of Bob. Daniel well knew that he was needed or he wouldn't have become involved in the situation in the first place.

But then again, to varying degrees, being needed is necessary to most people, the more so as they grow older. The tragedy of a lot of older gays, is that they don't know what they are needed for. They see themselves only as constant suppliants for the furtive pleasures of youth, without realizing that that youth may be confused, floundering, and as much in need as they are. Communication comes hard. The significance of *Sunday, Bloody Sunday* is that it shows such a relationship in action, and limns—at least partially—the interplay of need.

The interplay was evident on that gay boatride, when

I sat on the sidelines, tending the shirts, bags, and other accoutrements that Lamont and Vernon had left while they were out on the dance floor doing the Bump and other obscenities. First one and then the other would keep emerging from the melee to catch their breath, come and sit down next to me, put a hand on my knee, and just sit there, gasping. When they got their respiration under control, they'd be off again. They knew where I was. It was a reference point, a home base, and they kept touching it. They wanted it that way. I wanted it that way. I certainly didn't want to get up and make a fool out of myself on the dance floor. They didn't want to sit around on the sidelines. But the contact was constant, on their initiative, and was broken only when I went up on top deck to play my little time games.

I have had my troubles with the demons of possessiveness; it was the one thing they did not need, and could not tolerate. But authority was something else again. "You be in here by twelve midnight, or don't come back till morning." A statement like that they could understand and the likelihood would be that they'd be in by twelve. To me, it might be rank possessiveness, but to them, it was something to hang onto, the security of a flat statement, but with a choice. As long as they had the choice, odious as it might be, they didn't feel possessed.

Another strange thing. Sex they had like rabbits, but so many of them were starved for affection. Once they found a source of affection, they weren't at all bashful about asking for it. Like cats, they were always coming around to have their backs scratched. On the other hand, many of them found it difficult to give what they took. I remember one chilling story about a young gay who picked up an older gay in a bar and went back to his hotel room with him. Once they were undressed, the prospect of the night's exertions proved too much for the older man, and he had an attack of chest pain that was probably angina pectoris. The younger gay panicked, threw on his clothes, and left.

Hearing the story, I was outraged. "For Chrissake, the guy was in pain. He might even have died. So how come the kid runs out on him, leaves him alone?"

The argument got hot. "So what's he going to do, just hang around there to see if the guy's going to die, and then the cops come and all that jazz?"

"To hell with the cops. What about the guy?"

"So what about the guy? He's got heart trouble. It's not the kid's fault."

"He's got chest pain because he's all hyped up. Why couldnt' the kid have the decency to stay around and get him calmed down?"

"What do you mean?"

"Hold him, for God's sake! Just lie there beside him and hold him."

It was a new idea.

"Yeah, maybe he should have done that . . ."

It is no big secret that youth tends to be appallingly egocentric. Just as they have to stretch to expand their physical environment beyond their clothes, so they have to stretch to extend their emotional environments beyond their own skins. The stretch is all the more difficult in a transgenerational context because the adults with whom they habitually come in contact are all authority figures—parents, teachers, bosses, and cops—and authority figures tend, from a distance, to look armorplated. How do you empathize with a tank? Intellectually you may know that the person inside that armor plate is as vulnerable as anyone else. But the visceral response is to all that steel and that big gun of authority.

For younger gays, transgenerational communication is still more difficult because their reading of authority in the dominant straight culture tells them that they are "sick," "deviant," or what-have-you. Their internal reality is heavily at odds with the concepts that authority tries to impose on them, and the credibility of external authority is all the more strained. I heard it put succinctly: "I should have those nuts tell me I'm sick or crazy or something? Who do they think they're kidding?" The credibility of authority is still further strained by the fact that at least among some males in the dominant culture, public stances and private behavior don't always coincide: "So how come he's telling me what a bad boy I am, and cruising me at the same time?"

I guess, to a lot of the tribe, I was an authority figure. God knows, I made enough noise on occasion. But there was a difference. I wasn't imposed from the outside; I was discovered from the inside. I shared their condition and assumptions and they knew it. I talked freely about it. They could talk freely. They could come. They could go. Nobody had them chained to the bedpost. On the other hand, while they were here, responsibilities were put upon them. One of them drifted in one time after a couple of weeks' absence and crashed on the bed. Lying there in the darkness, he said, "You know, I miss you. Always telling me—do this, do that—I miss that."

But there was another factor in the situation. I certainly made no pretense of being invulnerable. This was, after all, my home. Not an office, or a classroom, or a precinct house. If I felt like getting mad, I got mad. If I felt I was being put upon, I said so, out loud—very loud. If I wanted to get drunk, I got drunk. If I wanted attention, I demanded it. A lot of the tribe had never had to deal with this kind of assertiveness, but at least they knew they were coping with another human being. Gradually they got the idea that if there really was another human being out there beyond their own skins, they had better pay it mind. As long as they were here, it was hard to avoid. Judging from the way they kept trooping back, they didn't seem all that anxious to avoid it. If I sounded like a professor of sociology at one moment and a demented old King Lear at another, it only seemed to increase the attraction.

I go into these dark details because, among other reasons, the relationship of Daniel and Bob in *Sunday, Bloody Sunday* was portrayed as so damn civilized! Okay, so they were two well-bred Englishmen and that's their problem. But I don't think older gays do any service to their juniors by trying to gussy themselves up into something they are not—emotionally, intellectually, or physically. Younger gays, if they are going to grow old with some grace, need to know what growing old is, with the bark off, and know it from people who are gay themselves.

I remember going with Vernon to see Visconti's film of Thomas Mann's *Death in Venice.* We sat there, looking at all those women's hats, interspersed with those outasight visions of Tadzio, and wallowed in the camp of it all. It was a crock, but a high-class crock . . . until that hairdresser started going to work on the older gay— Herr Professor—with the hair color and the makeup. Tarantulas started going up and down my spine. Suddenly the film was no longer camp. The final scene had Tadzio, the beautiful young boy, drifting off into some Whistler vision of the Adriatic, and Herr Professor sitting on a beach chair on the shore, dying, with the hair-coloring slowly dripping down his cheek.

Vernon giggled. I told him to shut up. Like a shot, he shut up. Walking out of the theater, I looked at him, and he looked at me, and he said, "Jesus . . ." And Vernon was only twenty-four.

I was brought up on Thomas Mann. I grew in my head because of him, but sometimes I wonder what else that man did to me. Did he tell me, in *The Magic Mountain,* that Settembrini and Naptha's courtship of Hans Castorp was a futile and impotent intellectual exercise, best conducted in the death environment of a tuberculosis sanitarium? Was he telling me in *Death in Venice* that a middle-aged intellectual could be utterly destroyed by some little adolescent cockteaser he pursued through the glittering decadence of Venice? Did he really believe that? Were the wellsprings of his own self-hate so deep that that was all he could communicate, and, in communicating through the power of his artistry, make others believe him? Is he, in fact, part of the culture that makes young gays want to die at thirty-five? Mann himself lived to a fulsome eighty or thereabouts, heavy with achievement and honor. If he could write about death in Venice, one wonders why he could not also have written about life in California.

Chapter Twelve

Most behavioral scientists and the preponderance of the general public seem to cherish the belief that homosexuality is a condition of arrested emotional and sexual development, caused by certain configurations within the family during the individual's childhood. This belief has led many psychiatrists to contend that, by taking the patient through a therapeutic process of one sort or another, they can "cure" him of his homosexuality.

This set of ideas is reassuring to the dominant culture. In those terms, homosexuality is a deviant condition or illness that can be remedied either by conventional psychotherapy or by such newer forms of behavioral intervention as aversion therapy. If Freud can't do it, Skinner can. These poor unfortunates can then be reunited with the norms of the culture.

These ideas, reassuring as they may appear at first

glance, bear a disturbing resemblance to the ideas that teachers in the nineteenth and early twentieth century had about children who wrote with their left hands. After all, the norm was right-handedness, and deviations from that norm were an offense against nature and the Deity. Hence all sorts of bizarre measures were tried to get these unfortunate children to write with their right hands, including tying the left hand behind the back during school hours. Happily it began to dawn on the teaching profession that maybe a left-handed child could learn to write as well as any other child if he or she was encouraged to be as good a left-handed penman as the other children were right-handed penmen. After that both child and teacher were spared a lot of anguish.

As more and more of the contradictions and fallacies of this belief in social conditioning as the primary cause of homosexuality become apparent, and as the sciences of biochemistry and genetics keep growing in sophistication, evidence and accompanying consensus is probably going to shift to the more reasonable concept that the proclivity to homosexuality is a biochemical constant in the human species, and that the only social intervention is recognition or nonrecognition of that constant. Once that change in conception takes place, we will all—gay and straight alike—be spared a lot of anguish.

At least we will have set aside both the primordial idea of gayness as "sin" and the current belief that it is a "curable illness." The setting aside of these two concepts will lead to the acceptance of gayness as simply a fact of human life which includes only one dysfunction —the disinclination (though not the incapacity) to have children. Considering the state of the world's population growth at present, this dysfunction does not seem as serious as it did when primitive tribal survival depended on fecundity—and when the concept of homosexuality as sin first emerged. Fecundity is not a very high social value these days. The disinclination to have children seems less of a "sin" than a virtue.

We can, I think, look forward to a substantive change in the public attitude toward homosexuality in the next generation; indeed, that change is already taking place. As all those closet doors swing open and the general public gets an idea not only of the prevalence but also of the caliber of the individuals who identify themselves as gay, that change in public attitude will accelerate.

Change in the public attitude toward gays will increase the range of options open to gays themselves. At first glance, it would seem that the most desirable option is complete integration, a general acceptance that a human being's sexual preference is his or her own business and no one else's, and a further acceptance that sexual preference is irrelevant to vocational and social functioning. But are gays themselves ready to accept this acceptance? How do gays themselves make the transition from impaired function in an oppressive society to full function in a liberated society? The obvious answer would seem to be to press for larger and still larger areas of integration. In other words, get into the general society and mix. This is precisely what a lot of gays are doing—as gays. But in the course of the year or so that this book covers, I found myself, for the first time, really beginning to understand those Black Separatists and those members of Women's Liberation who keep urging the sisters to get off by themselves and get their heads together. I developed a first-class dyed-in-the-wool ghetto mentality. I wanted to be with my own kind, and the consciousness of kind was gayness. When I wanted to walk, I'd walk on Christopher Street, not because I was cruising, but because Christopher Street was the place that most gays walked. In the summer the tribes gathered at the Morton Street pier. All year long we'd tolerate—indeed, rejoice in—conditions roughly analogous to the Black

Hole of Calcutta at sundry gay bars or at Firehouse dances. Gays, like many other minorities, like to herd, and the sexual implications of herding are implicit but frequently not primary. Reina, a queen I knew, after she lost her lover, spent nearly every evening for four months over at the Ninth Circle before she found herself a new stud. (It was proposed the day after that a large banner should be unfurled over the bar saying "You'll all be glad to know that Reina got laid last night.") But no one can tell me that Reina couldn't have found herself a stud in a hundred and one nights at the Ninth Circle; she went there for companionship, and if something came along, fine.

The various pasturages for herding were well defined, and so were the thistle patches. Right slam-dab in the middle of the gay activity in the Village was a curious establishment called Your Father's Mustache, which was dearly beloved of the swingingest of farm-equipment salesmen from central Kansas. No-o-o-body I knew ever went there! On weekend evenings, when there was sometimes a line out in front of Your Father's Mustache and the smell of new-mown hay was in the air, gays I knew would take some pleasure in walking slowly past the place hand-in-hand or arm-in-arm, pause at the corner, and go into some deathless swoon of an embrace— just to let the folks know whose territory it was. It was all kind of silly in a serious kind of way.

This urge to herd certainly runs counter to any abstract ideas of integration, but nevertheless I think it bodes well for Gay Liberation. Going out there and getting lost in the straight world seems at present almost as self-defeating as staying hidden in the closet. Gays need to get their heads together—together—and to enhance their sense of private identity that is the strength of their public identity.

I was over at Danny's dancing bar a couple of nights

ago and did a bit of wool-gathering, watching the people as they came down the stairs into the dance area. All the deer-people, and the giraffes, and the water buffalo, and the zebras, all coming down to the waterhole for a convocation and gathering at the place that was ineffably home turf. I was over at a street fair at the Firehouse recently on a rainy afternoon and had the same feeling. Superficial as it may be, I felt a warmth about the sheer fact of gathering, regardless of purpose or personal contact.

But sheer gathering for its own sake is obviously not enough. One of the most encouraging of all signs in Gay Lib is the development of homophile organizations on campuses throughout the United States in the past several years. At least it gives the gay community a corporate voice. But more important, it gives young gays an organizational turf and meeting place in a lot more serious context than the local gay bistro, tearoom, or what-have-you.

Consciousness-raising sessions, encounters, and other instrumentalities of the human potential movement also have an important role—I guess. I've detested the ones I've been to, but that's just one man's prejudice. They have a lot of satisfied customers, and if some of the sessions degenerate into out-and-out catfights, chalk it up to human frailty. I could imagine that for some young gay just coming out and beginning to cope with his own gayness, some kind of group sessions would be a godsend.

Political action has been the hallmark of the Gay Activist Alliance of New York. Leafleting, picketing, sit-ins, and other forms of political street theater all come under the general heading of Zapping the Straight Establishment, and as one GAA member put it, one good zap is worth a hundred hours on a shrink's couch. Now, admittedly, a good imaginative zap can cause acute discomfort to some political hack who thinks he's keeping "the faggots under control" by legally or extra-legally denying them elementary civil rights. Zaps are also catnip to the media, which, in turn, helps publicize the denial of those rights. But I can't help thinking that maybe one of the most important products of zapping is not political change but internal change in the people who are doing the zapping.

Peter Fisher, in his book *The Gay Mystique,* tells about his loneliness on first coming to New York, and then getting involved in GAA, "involved as I had never been involved in anything before." He found friends, "people with whom I was doing something I believed in," and he found his lover, Marc Rubin:

> I met Marc in GAA during the madhouse of the 1970 election activities. In the rush, excitement, and occasional righteous outrage of political confrontation, we drifted closer and closer together in the organization. We were together on the corner of Eighty-sixth and Broadway on a cold day, zapping a Democratic candidate. We were out for a beer with friends in the early morning after an interminable committee meeting. In November, we found an opportunity for a date together, got stoned, and held on to each other until *2001* took us off through the universe.

Certainly GAA is a lot more than a dating service. The point is a vital individual relationship grew out of an equally vital shared activity and the two vitalities intermingled.

A lot of vitalities in this society derive from function and the mutual reliance that comes out of shared function. It is probably just as well that most gays who have jobs have them in the straight world. A person can stand just so much ghettoization. Still, the development of functions within the gay subculture deserves some consideration. I don't mean social functions, necessarily, but services of many kinds to individuals and groups who are part of the scene.

Such a service infrastructure is beginning to emerge within the community. Newspapers like *Gay* and *The Advocate* provide a steady flow of information, news, and comment. Organizations such as the Mattachine Society, West Side Discussion Group, and GAA serve as clearing houses for information of various kinds, and the New York Mattachine Society maintains a comprehensive library of books and materials related to gay life. Troy Perry's Metropolitan Community Church in Los Angeles, and now in many other cities as well, has pioneered the ministry to gays, along with the Church of the Beloved Disciple here in New York. The activity in religion has led established church groups, like the Unitarians, to set up their own service ministries, which include both information and counseling.

GAA's Firehouse in New York has served as the center for a whole host of activities, including not only dances, but plays, film showings, bazaars (Kiss Holly Woodlawn for twenty-five cents!), consciousness-raising sessions, and those "interminable committee meetings" that Peter Fisher referred to.

Valuable as these services are, they are largely "soft" services requiring only a small amount of financing and related to social, religious, or personal needs. If we look for something with a commercial base to it that would provide an opportunity for an appreciable number of gays to work together, serve their own community, and earn a livelihood, there isn't much around. The bars employ gays right up to management level. So do the baths. What else? Various small retail operations, with three or four people involved. Summer resort community services at such gay enclaves as Fire Island. Some restaurants. But there is nothing much, really, that is distinctly gay, that employs and serves as gay. In the meantime a lot of young gays are vocationally floundering around in the straight world, taking menial jobs, working with people with whom they have few common interests, and frantically trying to hide their identity as gays.

Other gays gravitate to the theater, interior decorating, fashion, and other fields where gayness is accepted or at least tolerated. Still others go their solitary way, keeping their identity as gays hidden, until they get into a middle-management position in some business or institution, and then, with the best of intentions, start hiring kindred spirits until the accounting department, say, becomes known throughout the rest of the organization as "the Lavender Hill Mob." Such situations can get messy, because the hiring is done for reasons other than, say, accounting talent or experience, and because it is done sub rosa and Awaits Discovery, Viewings with Alarm, Quiet Conferences, and Departmental Shakeups.

Obviously sexual preference and life-style should be no more a factor in employment than left-handedness, and the pressure that GAA and other groups are putting on business organizations to see that gays get their vocational rights is crucial. Still, given the herding instinct that many gays have, and their interest in staying within the community, it seems appropriate that, in addition to pushing for vocational rights within the straight society, more allowance should be made and effort expended to provide vocational opportunity "at home," where gays can have functional working relationships as well as social and emotional ones.

Admittedly, this suggestion has a disturbing odor of prejudice-in-reverse about it. Should I discriminate, for instance, against a straight barber because there's a gay barber down the street? Well, come to think of it, I do.

Because I think he takes a little more care. If I had my druthers, I'd prefer a gay doctor because I'd feel more at ease talking with him. So what about a health clinic? Call it reverse prejudice, or call it the development of a community service infrastructure. All it really is, I guess, is a consciousness of kind.

Assuming that we are dealing here not with a social pathology but a biochemical constant, and assuming as well that with the evolution of the liberation movement, the prevalence of that constant will become publicly known and acknowledged, and finally assuming that consciousness of kind among gays themselves will grow, then I think a lot of consideration has to be given to the social, institutional, and economic forms through which that consciousness can express itself. In a diverse and polyglot society, gays are part of the mix, and instead of fretting about prejudice-in-reverse, perhaps it is better to acknowledge that ghettoization of a sort can be instrumental in creating a viable and creative subculture. If we want to herd, let's herd, but with a more coherent purpose than simply hanging together in the dark fastnesses of the local gay bar.

Perhaps one of the most important objectives in the development of the gay community, and the liberation that is implicit in that development, is the expansion of the employment opportunities for gays in the community service infrastructure. Just as blacks have brought heavy pressure to bear to increase black employment in black enclaves, both by setting up black businesses and by insisting on black employment in white-owned businesses serving the black community, so gays need to bring comparable pressure to bear in their own enclaves. As the opportunities continue to open up, some system needs to be established to see that those opportunities are known about, and are filled by people who have the will and skill to do the particular job. In other words, instead of the gay community being on the defensive, trying to maintain the rights of those who already have jobs, perhaps it would be wise, particularly within the enclaves where gays provide an appreciable segment of neighborhood economic activity, to go on the offensive on the basis of right-out-there-in-front gay identity.

The expansion of employment opportunity in the service sector of the economy, particularly in gay neighborhoods and enclaves, relates to the need of individual gays to have some sense of meaningful function and vocation—a work identity as well as an identity of lifestyle and sexual preference. The need is for a revitalization of that sense of vocation that seems a critical ingredient of the human personality.

But there's still a larger need, much more complex and difficult to respond to: the need of many gays to share in a functional working relationship that involves mutual reliance, as well as those general playing-around relationships that now seem to be the hallmark of the subculture. Without going into too great detail, what I'm suggesting is gay-owned and gay-operated businesses that can afford a variety of employment opportunities to gays of all ages to work in a sympathetic environment and that involves an interplay of skills, functions, and capacities focused on a corporate objective. In the past, businesses have been in the closet just as people have. Now it's time for gays to get their economic function as well as their personal identity up-front and out in the streets.

If this sounds antithetical to the great American ideal of the melting pot, consider that the melting pot is in fact a stew of discrete ingredients, and not an homogenized mush. Then the idea of kind-with-kind, sharing the same rights with other kinds-with-kind, is not unpalatable. In fact, it may be a lot better tasting.

The desirability of setting up gay-dominated work operations is one thing; the feasibility is something else again. First of all, on what scale? Obviously not major industry, which takes large amounts of capital and years of development. On the other side, let's forget operations employing a half-dozen people or fewer in a marginal business that may evaporate in a tremor of economic adversity. Let's concentrate on corporate functions involving the employment of anywhere from a dozen to a hundred people. A medical clinic for outpatients, such as has been described earlier in this chapter, would fall into that category. So would a gay community center. So would a fair-sized food store or restaurant. These might directly serve a gay community. But the social value of enterprises like this is not so much in service to the community as in providing a ready livelihood for gays, and the opportunity to share functional relationships. The product or service produced could be marketed anywhere to anyone.

What are the requirements? It would be best to have a mix of skilled and semi-skilled jobs. The enterprises would be heavy on labor use, with a comparatively low level of capitalization. A letter shop and duplication service is one possibility. Specialty garment manufacture is another. A franchise food distribution service (McDonald's, Baskin-Robbins, etc.) is also a possibility. Packaging and distribution of bulk products to retail outlets in a given area might also be explored. In each case, the enterprise might be started by older gays with basic management skills on the premise that younger gays would be hired for jobs requiring fewer skills, but with provision made for on-the-job training and systematic upgrading.

Those basic management skills, and a good business track record, which many closeted gays already have, is the key to financing. Lenders bet on markets; but more importantly, they bet on people. Of course, the classic business phraseology of "So, for 49 percent we're getting into bed with this guy" might acquire a more literal meaning; nevertheless the basic lender-entrepreneur relationshp is still there, based on the lender's trust in the entrepreneur's ability to manage and make money by whatever means (preferably legal) that the entrepreneur may opt for.

But the objective we are concerned with—providing employment for gays as such—might require some discretion. One can imagine some impeccable closet queen who works for an investment banking house or manages an investment trust making an informal and largely unspoken (let alone unwritten) understanding with some gay entrepreneur about just what was going on, but that that key understanding would not be shared with others concerned at the lending end of the deal. The agreement, as written, would simply be a straight business deal, standing on its own two feet. The entrepreneur's hiring policies would be his own business.

As long as the lending agreement reflected a valid chance for the investor to get a fair return for his money, there's nothing inherently dishonest about such a deal, and quite possibly, that is how some might be made. It wouldn't be the first time that unwritten understandings of that kind were determinative. Sometimes a wife's lily-white body gets wrapped in the package. Still, there's a stuffy closet smell about it that doesnt' befit a clear effort toward liberation. It's also worth bearing in mind that business investment of this kind is likely to be a long-term working arrangement, and if the man who made the original understanding is replaced, the new man on the lender's side is, quite pardonably, entitled to wonder just what in flaming hell he's gotten himself into here!

It seems a wiser long-range policy for the gay entrepreneur to be up-front and let it be known that whatever he is envisioning is going to be a gay operation, drawing its employees, provided they are qualified, from the gay community, just as black-dominated businesses give preference in hiring to blacks. If the enterprise requires rare skills, the investor has a perfect right to ask the entrepreneur what he's going to do if he can't find a qualified gay. If, on the other hand, the operation employs predominantly semi-skilled labor, then the entrepreneur is on much stronger ground in having a comparatively restricted employment policy—allowing, always of course, a place for the "house straight," just as military installations have a "base queen." Tokenism adds flavor, and would give gay employees a chance to say "Some of my best friends are straight, and I even work with one!"

An investor has a right to ask, as well, how the manager, after he has hired all these gays, intends to keep peace in the house. You can hear Mr. Moneybags muttering, "Christ, Harry, how are they going to get any work done? They'll be in each other's pants all day long!" Harry, being a tactful fellow, won't reply by pointing out that many secretaries and bosses don't keep out of each other's pants all day long, but manage still to turn out the day's work. But Moneybags has a point. In an industrial society, men and women have been working together for four or five generations and even though it's been a rocky road, *modi vivendi* and *modi operandi* have—to a certain extent—been established to maintain productivity. Gays have not had anywhere near the history or tradition of working together and the temptation to treat the working situation as an extension of the local gay bar may be considerable. Harry, the manager, might well find, after all the effort of financing and setting up an operation, and after the first flush of idealism in providing the brothers with a congenial means of livelihood, that in enforcing work discipline he has acquired a reputation as a reincarnation of Ivan the Terrible.

While functional working relationships among gays

usually don't have the formidable complexity of personal relationships that have a strong emotional component to them, still a considerable amount of thought needs to be given to codes of on-the-job behavior in which gays are right-out gays, free of the constraints imposed by a straight business establishment. There are no wars as bitter as civil wars; no discord so abrasive as among kindred. The very sense of kind among gays could, under the pressure of a working situation, lead to conflicts so intense that they could seriously jeopardize a given area of productivity. It is important to try to head off an incipient conflict before it has a chance to reach a crisis stage. Some people just can't work together, and the sooner these incompatibilities are recognized, the better. Otherwise the operation is likely to be affected by one of those long, slow, grinding hostilities that can affect the morale of everyone around. On the other hand, I've noticed one attribute among the gays I've known that may be encouraging—a really remarkable capacity to bury the hatchet after sudden, explosive, and vituperative conflict. The storms can come with window-rattling ferocity, but as quickly as they come, they go. One day it's "I never want to see that son-of-a-bitch again, no way!" But the next day it's "Oh, well, what the hell, he's all right, I guess." And off they go down the street, arm in arm. I suppose you could say it's all in the family. But I don't know whether that general pattern of social behavior would carry over into a working situation or not. After all, in a social situation, the two parties in conflict can get away from each other for a while and cool off. But with the discipline of a job to be done, there's no getting away until quitting time. An open question.

Then there's the matter of goofing off—soldiering on the job, absenteeism, and other manifestations of bone-laziness. The problem is not unknown in general industry and business, and the relationship of alcoholism to depletions in productivity is startling. Industrial workers develop good work habits, and then get drunk to forget them. The problem with the younger gays I've known is somewhat different; they've never developed good work habits in the first place. In their chaotic lives, socialization is primary. Since their economic needs aren't that great, income production is secondary. Providing economic support for a wife and children is, for the straight male, a sobering obligation, and leads him to value job stability, upgrading, fringe benefits, and pensions. If, in his middle years, he hits the bottle as a protest against his captivity, count it as an aberration from an established life-plan, the continuity of which passes on to his children. But what's the job motivation for a young gay who never intends to have a family and who has the conviction that he's probably going to die by the time he's thirty-five? A pension? You've got to be kidding! Just give me the cash, Jack, so I can get a new body suit or take off for Puerto Rico.

Maybe that is a valid way to live. Quite possibly all the future-directed, security-minded, goal-oriented striving that passes as "career development" and is likely to lead to an early grave from coronary disease or an utterly meaningless "retirement" to some geriatric warren in Florida is one of the unhappy delusions of the dominant culture, designed to enhance the material productivity of the economy and grind individuals to pulp in the process. But still, it's a pretty gruesome spectacle to see some poor queen in her forties trying to eke out a living dog-walking poodles for her friends, or sales-clerking at some small gay boutique that can barely support the owner. Sure, she has her memories of all those body suits and trips to Puerto Rico, but now . . .?

Some years ago I was a department head of a modest-sized outfit in San Francisco and had occasional job-openings to fill, usually copy jobs. But whether or not I had any openings, a steady stream of applicants, three or four a week, would check the office out for possibilities. Almost without fail they were deer-people in their thirties or forties who had worked (and some of them had pretty good résumés) in New York, and had finally saved up enough money to buy that plane ticket and cut out for San Francisco! They'd usually have enough money stashed to maintain themselves for a month or so while they found a job and established themselves in the good gay life of the Queen City of the West.

The problem was that there were damn few jobs.

I'd sit there, old Straight-Arrow himself, and try to explain to the brothers that San Francisco was simply an overgrown branch town trying to act like a city and that, if they wanted to get where the vocational action was, they should head for Los Angeles. Better I should have told them to leave for Scranton, Pennsylvania. They wanted San Francisco, and the decision didn't have one damn thing to do with "vocational action," it had to do with the fact that the Wagner administration was doing its venomous best to make life miserable for gays in New York City and that San Francisco was a liberated refuge area. I wonder how many of those poor brothers, whose qualifications might have stood them well in Los Angeles, Chicago, or Philadelphia, ended up washing dishes at the Blue Fox or the Black Cat.

All right, what does Gay Liberation mean in terms of this present-day vocational dishevelment? For one thing, we can fairly assume that no municipal administration in a major metropolitan area is going to try to pull the same shenanigans that the Wagner administration pulled in New York in terms of entrapment, raids, and the general use of policemen as a bedroom brigade. Liberation has meant the growth of political power of the gay community nationwide, and we are simply not going to stand for that shit anymore. As much as reasonable job security, a gay has a right to his own life-style in the urban area where he earns his livelihood, and should not have to uproot his vocational life just because some pinheads in City Hall conclude that he has no right to exist.

The liberation movement involves not only the job security issue, which has been emphasized by GAA, but also, as pointed out earlier in this chapter, the expansion of employment opportunities for gays, as gays, and the setting up of gay-dominated businesses and institutions for those gays who want to work as well as live within the subculture. But even if all these components of external liberation are in some appreciable measure achieved, the process of internal liberation is the special province and responsibility of the gay community itself.

One time I had the task of boiling down a hundred hours of taped interviews with California Indians into four thirteen and a half-minute radio programs. The California Indians were a pretty sad crew who, before the coming of the whites, spent a lot of time digging for acorns and going through interminable "white deer-skin" dances. The whites pretty well wiped them out, and about the only time they hit third gear was with Captain Jack in the Modoc Wars, when they stood off a fair segment of the American Army in the lava beds of Northern California. After that it was downhill all the way, with demoralization setting in like a Sierra snowfall.

In interview after interview, tape after tape, the point was made and made again that the children of these Indian families simply weren't hacking it either in school or in urban resettlement off the reservations because their parents were so demoralized themselves that they could see little reason to offer their children any encouragement to get out there and push. The family couldn't seem to provide incentive; it just kept retrogressing to digging acorns. When the children were subjected to even the rudimentary complexities of schooling, let alone the realities of urban life, they couldn't cope, and many of them went "back to the blanket," i.e., the reservation. The intergenerational transmission system, implicit in family life, that endows youngsters with a culture, tradition, and the psychic identity had broken down. The families neither believed in their past nor hoped for a future, and the children were left . . . nowhere.

California Indians are a depressing analogue, but the comparison has a point. Without a transmission system, you can neither get a culture off the ground nor keep it moving, nor expect it to respond to changing conditions. I keep wondering if the floundering around of younger gays within the subculture and the pervasive lack of motivation that might lead to a real vocation cannot be attributed in large measure to the fact that the gay community does not have a transmission system that works. Like the California Indians, the younger gays, "the children" of the gay community, are left . . . nowhere. And also, like the California Indians, the older people of the community, bearing the weight of a tradition of centuries of oppression, are also . . . nowhere. Doesn't it seem reasonable to suggest that if we could build an intergenerational transmission system that works, both groups might get . . . somewhere?

Gays, like everyone else, come out of a family environment. But once they step across the line into the gay subculture, that original family environment, for a variety of reasons, is likely to lose its central place in their consciousness. The transition is in one sense analogous to the young straight getting married. They both leave the nest. But the young straight goes *to* someone—his wife. The young gay goes into the general swirl of the subculture where there are few polarities, few guidelines to behavior beyond a vague but emerging consensus among peers based largely on the necessities for survival. Pretty thin stuff, that. Past and future—the effect of past history on present action, the effect of present action on future being—these critical time-linkages seem tenuous in their minds, maybe because there are so few people around to remind them. Yet it is just those linkages that give coherence to a life: vocationally, socially, and emotionally.

But if cultural transmission within the subculture doesn't work very well now, we can fairly assume that as liberation progresses, we will have an opportunity to explore and experiment with various forms and modes of transmission that can give the culture stability and the individuals in it a clearer perspective of themselves and their social environment.

Both the tribal and one-to-one transmission systems need more form than they have now, more thought needs to be given to them, more acknowledgment to their significance in the development of the gay community as a whole. And that means that a lot more closet doors are going to have to swing open.

In early 1973, the president of GAA got a phone call from a man who, after introducing himself, mentioned that he had been a high official of the New York State Employment Service. He noted that he was now retired, on a pension, and beholden to none. I'm gay, he said, and I want to help. What can I do? When that conversation was reported at a Thursday night general meeting, you should have seen the expression on the faces of younger gays in that audience!

Chapter Thirteen

A large-scale and diverse culture, such as we see here in the United States, strengthens and enhances itself by drawing distinctive contributions from its component subcultures. As the process of liberation continues, the gay subculture is invigorated, and interchange between gays and straights is freer, it seems valid to ask what gays have to contribute not only to their own community development, but to the national eco-system.

In the past the contribution has, I think, been relatively minor. Some words have seeped up from the gay underground into general usage. Men and women's fashions have been affected by gay tastes. Theater and interior design frequently have a gay imprint. But while these contributions may decorate, they do not necessarily enhance, strengthen, or enlarge the dimensions of the culture as a whole.

More significantly, as Lesbians have played a crucial and catalytic role in the development of Women's Liberation, gay males have an equally significant role to play in the liberation of the straight male. *Not,* it should be emphasized, by trying to "convert" him to gayness, but rather by helping him unburden himself of the bondages that have been put upon him, so that he can be free in the dimensions of his own nature. Gays have had some experience with that struggle.

I recently saw the play *That Championship Season* and since it has some cogent things to say about the current status of the American male, it is worth discussion.

Four macho jocks in their late thirties who, twenty years before had won the Pennsylvania high school basketball championship, get together with their macho coach for a reunion one evening and proceed to booze it up for old times' sake. As in the case of plays like *Who's Afraid of Virginia Woolf?* and *Boys in the Band,* the shit hits the fan. Everybody ends up looking at themselves and at each other (excepting, in this case, the coach) with that terrible knowledge of middle-aged disenchantment and dishevelment that singes their already shriveled spirits. All they are left with is the memory of one moment of excellence—when they won the championship (and even that proves tarnished)—and each other. What follows is a scene of love among men so powerful that it makes *Boys in the Band* sound like queen patter. Embedded in the center of that scene is a statement of one of the players, who is staring at the two-foot-high silver cup that the team won that championship season: "I don't believe in trophies anymore."

The statement is all the more reverberant because the coach spends the evening reciting all the homilies of American Success, with special reference to that old trophy-hunter Teddy Roosevelt. The rejection of trophies marks a profound cultural transition in this country's consciousness, a transition from the faith that enough macho and virile gumption can solve any problem, surmount any challenge, to another state of consciousness. Gayness has a role to play in that transition, as indeed it was central to the play on stage. When all else, themselves included, failed, they at least could stick together and were drunk enough to express their love for one another. And that was their redemption. As it may be the redemption of this frazzled, confused country, whose sense of macho invincibility has led it not only to impotence, but to crimes unspeakable. We have believed in trophies.

In various societies men and women see themselves differently, and act differently. As societies change, so do these self-images, and from these images come new patterns of relationship that establish a new ordering of cultural life. Once the change has taken place, historians and behavioral scientists can go back over the circumstances that provided the context for the change and spot not only how the change took place, but some of the reasons why.

In the history of medieval Europe, for instance, there is one suggestive example of change of male self-image, the emergence of chivalric consciousness. Looked at in retrospect, the whole idea of the gentle knight, living a code of honor, bravery, and loyalty, seems rather arcane. Historians have found plenty of evidence that the chivalric code was more honored in the breach than in the observance, and that the phenomenon itself was probably a product of "media imagination"—in medieval terms, the shamans and romancers. But looked at from the vantage point of, say, Western Europe in the seventh century, with those Merovingians in France pulling each other apart with horses, and the Angles and Saxons, all decked out in bearskins, hunting down and killing every Celt they could find, the emergence of chivalric man looks better all the time! I mean, those people in the seventh century were really troglodytes to whom My Lai slaughters were a way of life and a statement of virility. No code. No sense of themselves as anything other than pure predator. And probably less sense of cooperation and mutual dependence than the average wolf pack.

It is obvious in retrospect that what we know as "Western Civilization" was not going to get off the ground until the males of the society got their heads together. And, yes, there was a lingering memory of "civilization," not only in the historic Judaism described in the Old Testament, but in imperial Rome, an idea that Charlemagne, in his primitive way, tried to revive in the latter part of the eighth century. But the emergence of chivalric man depended not so much on memories of past societies as past men—primarily Arthur and Roland, whose exploits were legend, and as the legends were enhanced in the telling and retelling, their characters grew to heroic proportions that were the models for a new kind of male aspiration. Powerful and virile, yes, but also gentle and generous. The memory of those two men, Arthur and Roland, can arguably be considered the ultimate ancestry of everything we now call civilized male behavior. Yet the concept of chivalric behavior was, in the twelfth and thirteenth centuries, a major change in how men saw themselves, and regardless of countless breaches of the code, how they generally acted. In time, the gentle knight was to become the gentleman, but the code was still there. In our own time, we have known Camelot.

In a remarkable article, "Gay Is Good for Us All" by Suzannah Lessard, which first appeared in the *Washington Monthly* (and has subsequently been reprinted in the *Homosexual Dialectic*), there is a description of the Christopher Street Day parade up Sixth Avenue in June of 1970, the "first big holiday from the closet." Ms. Lessard

rightly sees that march as the first large-scale, organized
public assertion of a liberation movement that, along
with Women's Lib and Black Lib, constitutes a revolu-
tionary challenge to the "white male heterosexual king
who sits in the throne room, guarding his birthright."

Ms. Lessard sees that "king" with as clear eyes as play-
wright Jason Miller sees him in *That Championship Season*.
She writes:

> The faces of men commuting on trains between
> affluent suburbs and their high-level work in the
> big-time world of the city are blank and worn
> beyond their years. They don't seem like people in
> the flush of fulfillment, and the inheritors of the
> earth, or for that matter like cruel, arrogant nobles
> gripped with the excitement of power. They sit on
> the train wrapped in their newspapers, for a spell
> excused from guarding their titles, and they seem in
> this rare unselfconscious moment a tired dreary lot.
> It would seem that rather than possessors they
> themselves are the spoils of kingship.

She goes on to ask a question that has undoubtedly
occurred to many cardiologists and psychiatrists: "Isn't
the throne room as vicious a dungeon of [the king's]
humanity as those in which he keeps his underlings?"

Noting that in their early stages liberation movements
have been afflicted with the "self-seriousness, ambition
and assertiveness" that are characteristic of "the king,"
himself, Ms. Lezzard calls for a "redirection of energies
from a drive to parallel the white male oppressor into an
effort to evolve a whole new image of man and society
which will change things for the better for everybody,
including Massah King." With the fusion of the various
liberation movements, she sees society moving toward
"the ideal of a world built according to human needs

rather than according to power. The redefinition of those needs is a far greater revolution than any straight political rearrangement could, in itself, accomplish." As for the king himself, he will be liberated "when the whole pack of role cards falls—when he is not restricted by the king-male role." She foresees that "when more men feel that they no longer need to be the king-male—or share his compulsive desire to be crowned, to reign virile and proud and appreciated—maybe there will be fewer bloodied people, fewer good things ravaged, and maybe even fewer wars."

Far-fetched? Think about those two macho types, Johnson and Nixon, and the Vietnamese. Think about the perhaps apocryphal statement—"Ho Chi Minh told me 'chickenshit.' Nobody tells Lyndon Johnson 'chickenshit' and gets away with it!" And on the bombing went. Well, it's sort of a Zane Grey version of chivalric honor, foreign policy out of an old Gary Cooper movie. At least it's an improvement over the Merovingians. But the "improvement" is just not sufficient unto the day. It is as unlikely that we can make a more humane society out of old Gary Cooper movies as it was unlikely that the Merovingians could make a coherent society out of chaotic barbarism. The Zane Grey mentality may have built the West, but it is doubtful that it can conserve humankind or respond to human needs, in any contemporary sense. People caught in power serve power's ends. Even though there may be some chivalric amelioration of the raw exercise of power, "the king," in Ms. Lessard's terms, is still locked in his dungeon throne room. As long as he sees himself as "king," he is a prisoner there.

Maybe the whole point of *That Championship Season* is that those poor-slob jock "kings," for a small luminous time, broke out of the throne room and, in a booze-induced freedom, besported themselves as themselves—weak, frightened, desolate, grasping, loyal, and loving.

On the train, perhaps, they'd be a "tired, dreary lot." But drunk at their old coach's house, call them the raw material for a new order of manhood.

I've gotten some shadowy ideas of what that new order might be by watching what went on around me, and by watching the changes that went on in myself. Teddy Roosevelt rated pretty high in my upbringing, too. There was his statue, right outside my favorite childhood hangout—New York's Museum of Natural History. Teddy astride his big horse, with a poor African afoot to one side, and a poor Indian afoot on the other. Teddy was obviously leading "the lesser breeds without the law" into the ways of White Enlightenment, and by sheer force of his macho virility saving the world. I thought that was a pretty fine statue when I was a kid. By God, that Roosevelt was a *man,* high in his stirrups on his big horse, a man who could take responsibility, a man who could lead, a man who could dare and prevail. He was a Kipling Hero, and no matter that Kipling had also written a "Recessional."

A couple of weeks ago I went back to the Museum of Natural History with one of the tribe. On our way in, we were confronted with The Statue. He stopped and gawked. I stopped and gawked. Then he looked at me saucer-eyed and pointed. "Who the hell is *that* idiot?"

The change of vision, as far as that statue was concerned, was complete. What had been highly impressive to me once was now hilarious satire, all the more so for being unintentional. That was no man up there on that horse; it was a cartoon.

The guy I was with kept looking at the statue, shaking his head. "You know, Johns like that," he said clinically, "most of them have a hard time getting their rocks off, and some of them like to wear women's panties."

I protested that Roosevelt had had a large and lively family, that, to the best of my knowledge, he let his wives wear the panties, and had been onto the ecology thing a couple of generations before he had been born.

The guy continued to shake his head. "The cat's a macho freak. You still find them around. A lot of them are black these days." He shrugged. "They'll get over it."

I kept watching myself get over it. The process was not so much gay as Aquarian, a kind of unfolding of empathy that came very gradually, unmarked by any particular moments of stark revelation or enlightenment. Consciousness III has come slow.

I've spent so damn much time in throne rooms, if only as a minor courtier, playing out the rigidities of roles and rituals! It was fun, cherishing all those little tokens of power, playing the chips of policy and program, funding and operation. To be predatory was to feel the flow of androgens, the assurance of power was a reassurance of self. I could get pretty high in the stirrups, seeing things happen that I had made happen. That I had done what I thought was valid was only part of the story. The other part was that, by whatever force it took, I'd done it. But in the process? I could shrug that off. Other people were there, all right, and given their due, as befits throne-room protocol. It's just they weren't all *that much* there for me. After all, how much thereness do you want when the game is ritual?

But now . . . Role? Protocol? Ceremony? What are they? All that's real is thereness.

The thereness is often most real in utter silence. I'll haul myself out of bed in the morning to hit the type-writer, sit there with a cup of coffee and a cigarette, staring at the wall and growling softly at the prospect of the day's work, when there is a knock at the door. One of the tribe, after a night of debauch, comes in to crash. It isn't a practice I encourage, but turning away some stoned, exhausted guy, even though the exhaustion is of his own making, isn't something I find easy to do. So, okay, crash.

As the day wears on, I'll prowl the apartment. There, on the waterbed pillow, is a tousled mass of hair. Turning, a face in sleep, and the outline of a body under the covers. He'll stretch himself in some disquieted sprawl, then curl himself in a ball against the world, then straighten to lie full length, his hands folded across his chest in serenity, then turn on his side and embrace a pillow for some surrogate comfort, and finally sprawl again, this time with flung abandon.

Strange how I feel his thereness, even sitting at the typewriter with him not visible, feel a sense of brooding, standing watch, a sense of empathy with the dramas he's playing out in sleep. They are his storms and serenities, but mine, too. The thereness is hereness and they meld in being. I never felt that way before.

Mid-afternoon and time to get him up. Sometimes it is quite a process, first stirring the waves of the waterbed and watching him float up and down, then bringing wakeful reality nearer with a shake of the shoulder, and seeing him stir. I start talking, slow and steady, as if I'm taking him down off an acid trip. He moves in the fluidity of the waterbed. His eyes flicker, open, find mine in vague focus, then sharper. He smiles and stretches himself. His hand rests on mine for a moment, then slowly he pushes himself out of the waterbed, stands there in the daylight, body and soul.

That's all. Just a guy, roused out of sleep from the womblike waterbed. Or am I watching a birth of a new kind of man?